Around The World In Thirty Years:

Just For A Start

Around The World In Thirty Years:
Just For A Start

CHRIS HYDE

CONTENTS

FOREWORD   7

ONE: THE VILLAGE, THE FOREIGNER AND "HARD"   9

TWO: CHRISTMAS, SKIS AND DODGER   17

THREE: THE RAINFOREST, MBA AND THE GREVE   25

FOUR: NUNS, NUTS AND NARCOSIS   36

FIVE: MORPHING, NEFTYANIKS AND INVOICES   49

SIX: THE MAMBA, THE BADGER AND DINNER   59

SEVEN: CONTRACTORS, ROTTWEILERS AND MURDER   69

EIGHT: NUTS, GRASS AND SHIT   83

NINE: DETENTION, BURHANS AND IBUPROFEN   93

TEN: I'M NOT MUCH BETTER WITH PLANES   107

ELEVEN: BEATING A BASTARD, GARBAGE AND FENCES   121

TWELVE: TRUMPETS, TEHRAN AND TERRIFIED   135

THIRTEEN: BEER, BUSSES AND BALLS OF FIRE   150

FOURTEEN: FILTERS, FINES (AND SOME MORE FINES)   165

FIFTEEN: ADJECTIVES, ADVICE AND CAPTAIN AHMED   179

THE END   196

THE WORLD (SIMPLIFIED)

SIBERIA

KAMCHATKA

METRO MANILA

NORTH SEA OIL RIG

WEST

FRIESLAND

IRAN

OMAN

DHAKA

AFRICA

EGYPT

GABON'ISH

WEST

YORKSHIRE

MAJORCA

MARK TWAIN

Foreword

IT'S MY FIRST recollection of feigning complete confidence whilst bullshitting. A handy talent that I practiced and perfected. At my interview with Oil & Gas Inc., leaving University with a shiny new maths degree, they said, "… are you applying for Oil & Gas Inc. International or Oil & Gas Inc. UK?". I didn't know. Was there an O & G Inc. International? It sounded outside of Yorkshire. I'd been to Majorca for a week and that had been alright. So why not. "International, of course".

In a comprehensive school in Yorkshire, in the 1970s, hard to imagine living and working in the deserts of Oman, the rainforest of French speaking Gabon, the traffic of Metro Manila, the attitudes of Friesland, the bomb craters of Iran, the deltas of West Africa, the winters in Siberia or the toilets in Egypt's Western Desert. And a few other places in passing.

I can do jet lag quite well, but I must have learnt something else along the way.

I was on a North Sea oil rig at New Year 1988. Six months after Piper Alpha killed 167 people. It was a tense time offshore. More tense if you had family working there. I was on night shift. At midnight I was crawling around inside a small ventilation duct, with a bag of spanners, fixing something. I crawled out later looking like a Victorian chimney sweep. I phoned my Mum to wish her Happy New Year. She asked what I'd been doing at midnight and I told her. In the way that only mothers can, she asked, "Did you need a degree to do that?" She had a point. It was quite prophetic really – she was predicting the rest of this book.

In Russia, I'd go to the gym every morning. It was in my work calendar. "Meeting with gym". 10am every day. I wasn't skiving – it was thinking time. I was a better person after I'd been running or cycling. I'd come back to the office and say to my PA, "Olga, I've had an idea" and her face would collapse. It was usually a good idea, but it did mean work. Often for her.

So, this book was born on a dozen different treadmills, and grew up during thousands of kilometers running, cycling or swimming, whilst remembering weird events, replaying odd conversations and recalling personalities. And there's lots more – you'll be glad to know. Some poignant. Some instructional.

I must have read Mark Twain as a kid, "Never let the truth get in the way of a good story", and I don't. These recollections could be 99% truth or 99% fiction – it is one or the other. You decide.

In my warped world, this book's funny. You might think it's full of laddish behaviour and immature humour. And you'd be right. But until you are cold, tired, hungry, far from home, on your thirtieth straight day of 16 hour working, under pressure, frightened and pissed off – as you are frequently in the oilfield – don't judge. Just enjoy.

CHAPTER ONE

The Village, The Foreigner and "Hard"

SALYM WAS JUST what you imagine from a poor, isolated village in forgotten Western Siberia.

Four feet of snow from November to April, minus 50 in February, plus 30 and mosquitos the size of birds in August. Wooden log huts for houses. Long drop toilets the norm. Old ladies called Ludmilla or Olga, in big boots, scarves, and fur coats, pulling sledges of shopping back from the only grocery store. No obvious reason for Salym to be there unless you traced the history of the gulags, the development of the timber industry and the building of the trans-Siberia railroad.

And the people were hard. They'd survived Stalin, several wars, Perestroika and the winter that happened every year. The hardest of the hard was the mayor, Vitaly Yurovich.

The villagers called me the "Innostrannik" – the foreigner. I'd been sent there to build and run an oil field on their doorstep. I had 5993 Russians, many from out of the region – from the 'Stan states - and 7 or so Westerners. Only me involved with the local community really – charged with making sure we genuinely did the right thing. For many, at that time, I was the only foreigner they'd spoken to.

I'd got a reputation for taking on the frontier locations. The Field Manager in these places is the town and county planner, judge and jury, fire chief, local health authority, headmaster, cash register, mediator in chief, emergency service, entertainment secretary, local authority schmoozer, whipping boy, power supplier, road builder, provider of water, sewage and food. In spare time, also the producer of oil and the maintainer of everything. Freely available 6am to 10pm, outside of those hours by appointment only. Or by emergency call. Anywhere you have thousands of people living in a closed environment, there are no boundaries to the problems, and they all walk into your office at some point. It wasn't easy. But it was often fun. And it's led to this book.

Just different rockets.

Vitaly Yurovich called me "drooziya" – friend, and meant it. And vice versa. For whatever reason, we hit it off – we had a mutual respect and easy friendship that you couldn't expect from two people with such different backgrounds and no common language. I was there for 6 years. He welcomed me into the traditions, the frustrations and the celebrations of the village – it was a privilege to be there and have that insight into a world so distant from my own. I grew up in small town North Yorkshire in the 70's, went to comprehensive school, took no interest in languages or culture, and hid under the desk with everyone else, when they showed the film of Cold War Russian rockets targeting the west. Vitaly and I are about the same age, so I guess he was in remote Siberia, doing much the same things, under a desk that looked much the same as mine, at much the same time. Just different rockets.

30 years later and I was in Khanty Mansysk district breathing Russian air, wearing a fur hat and genuinely in awe of the talented and welcoming Russian people that I was living and working with.

THE MAYOR, THE HAT AND THE GROANING

No Russian tradition is more important than the "banya". It's too simple to say that the banya is a Russian sauna. It's an institution, more like the village pub in England. In every village the first building, the most valued building and the best building is the banya. Historically, villagers used the banya not just as a sauna, but for washing themselves and their clothes and as a social hub. When it's minus 50, all of that takes on more of an importance. Being wooden, and heated by burning wood, they burn down frequently – but building something bigger and better would start before the fire stopped, and the new one would be, well, bigger and better. Until that burnt down.

… they burn down frequently ….

Public banyas in cities have a dodgy reputation. The implication being a bit like going to an inner-city massage parlour in the UK. Saunas are not big in North Yorkshire and not much above the dentist, in my eyes, as a social event. So, when Vitaly phoned my PA and interpreter, inviting me to his house for dinner with his family, and an evening with him in his banya, I wasn't totally thrilled.

I didn't speak much Russian in those early months, and Vitaly no English, so when my PA said she'd translate over dinner, but no way she was going anywhere near the banya, I

11

braced myself for a bit of weird.

Vitaly had the best house in the village. His banya was across his vegetable patch, 50m from his home and only slightly smaller. It was a treat for me to escape the oilfield for an evening, and a huge mark of respect, that I'd been invited – so when, shortly after arriving at his place, Vitaly took me to his banya, I was just happy to soak in this unlikely companionship.

The first room in the banya was like a living room – carpet, settee, tv, fridge – a curtained window onto the vegetable patch. Vodka is the drink of choice for the banya, with beer considered a soft drink and compot for the children. I had a genuinely zero tolerance policy towards alcohol in my field. I was returning there that night, so it was compot for me – a kind of natural mixed fruit juice. It was a mark of the respect we had for each other, that Vitaly didn't try badgering me into drinking with him – that would have been normal between two Russians. In deference to me, Vitaly was on Baltica – the standard Russian beer at that time. Baltica 2, 4, 6 and 10. The number being the alcohol percentage. One litre bottle of Baltica 10 and any normal European would be horizontal, a second bottle and you were on the way to casualty.

We watched TV for ten minutes and talked in pigeon Russian and sign language. Vitaly stood up and gave me a towel. It had a bit of Velcro down one edge. I guessed I was supposed to take off my clothes and put on this toweling skirt. By the time I'd got my shirt off, Vitaly had stripped off, put on his toweling skirt and had disappeared somewhere. But I'd missed an important detail. I had a dilemma only a Yorkshireman in a banya can have … was it underpants off, or underpants on … and yes, with hindsight, it was obvious. I decided it was underpants off, and I'd just got the skirt on when Vitaly came back. Not wanting to get this wrong, in my best, but still truly shit Russian, with most of the useful words missing, I tried asking him the underpants question. Realising my dilemma, but without the words to answer, he just opened his toweling skirt, pointed at where his underpants were not, and laughed.

Wanting to re-assure him that I'd understood, I just opened my toweling skirt in a Benny Hill'esque flash, and pointed. I'd just shown the local mayor my genitals. I was used to weird, but this was going to be something else.

... without the words to answer, he just opened his toweling skirt ...

We went through into the "cool room" – I didn't know it was only the cool room, I thought this was it. This was a more spartan room – unfinished wooden walls, no windows, no furnishings, but what I can only describe as a wooden double bed minus any mattress, headboard or pillows. A selection of buckets and some bunches of birch twigs and that was it.

We laid down on the double bed and chatted a bit more. I was obviously going to get to know the mayor in ways I couldn't have imagined. Very convivial, but not knowing any better, it looked like this was it. I couldn't really see what all the fuss was about. It wasn't even that hot.

A few minutes later, and he took me through into the hot room – a tiny, dark room with wooden bench seating and a big steel furnace that was burning one small forest each hour. Now it was hot. I was hoping there weren't any more rooms.

At a certain point he gave me a white pointy felt hat – somewhere between klu klux klan and Robin Hood. It couldn't get much weirder, so I put it on. As did Vitaly – his had his name on it – I suppose in case I got confused about who he was. I checked mine in case I'd got the one with "twat" written on it.

I checked mine in case I'd got the one with "twat" written on it.

He gave me two birch leaves – dipped his own two leaves in a bucket of water – and stuck one on the outside of each nostril. All self-respect gone; I did the same. The hat is supposed to stop your hair singeing and the wet leaves mean you only get second degree burns on your nostrils.

I had that vision of Blackadder with underpants on his head and pencils up his nose, to avoid going "over the top" in World War One. And I wondered if I was ok. It was hot – which is the point I suppose – so I was glad when we went back through to the cool room after 5 minutes or so.

I laid down on the double bed with Vitaly, bollock naked apart from a towel skirt, a pointy felt hat and two leaves stuck on my nose and wondered where this was in my job description. We chatted a bit, I thought it had been quite pleasant but had kind of expected there'd be more to the banya ritual than that. And wasn't it time for dinner.

After 5 minutes, Vitaly took off his toweling skirt and I worried what was next. And off he went back into the furnace – so I did the same. I'd done quite a lot of work with local governments in different parts of the world – but this was a first. Once in, he gave me a bundle of birch twigs. Soaking the birch twigs in a bucket of hot water, he started whipping his back and his thighs. It couldn't get any weirder – so I did the same, vaguely thinking that when I got back to the field I'd adopt a "what goes in the banya, stays in the banya" policy.

It was quite pleasant, and really hot, which was still the point I suppose.

Ten minutes of that and we were back in the cool room – tipped a couple of buckets of iced water over our heads, gasped a bit and had another little lie down tete-a-tete. Bollock naked, not even the towelling skirt, back on the double bed, with the mayor of Salym. Not forgetting funny hat and leaves on the nostrils, skin slightly raw from some self-flagellation, wondering what was happening to my guts with the gallons of prune juice I was guzzling. I did maths and engineering at University. It had taught me how to calculate pipe stress, and do a bit of engineering ethics, but I must have missed the module on doing weird shit in weird places.

Still it had been quite nice, my skin did feel good, I'd experienced the banya and dinner must be just about there.

Ten minutes later and we were back in the furnace – this time Vitaly got me to lie face down on the top tier of the benches where it was now REALLY FUCKING HOT. It wasn't as dark anymore because of the glow from my superheated nose. Out of the corner of my eye, I saw him pick up a bunch of birch twigs, and then I saw him put on a glove. Possibly delirious, it was impossible not to think of a prostate exam. Is a rummage in your prostate really a traditional part of the banya experience? I was just having that thought, when Vitaly whacked me on the back with the birch twigs and then dragged them down my back, whilst pressing hard with his gloved hand. He had my attention. The glove was protecting Vitaly's delicate Siberian hand from the superheated birch twigs, but nothing was protecting my delicate Yorkshire back. A close run thing between that and a prostate exam, for a good night out.

The next time Vitaly whacked me, and started dragging the birch twigs down my back, pressing hard with the gloved hand, he let out this long, low, animal groan. I was just thinking of giving him first aid for whatever pain he was in, when I twigged – sorry – that this is part of the ritual.

I wondered if I should be doing the groan.

For the next few minutes, I was checking the room for webcams and undercover reporters from The Telegraph, mentally writing a strongly worded email to my boss and wondering if I had a good case for a bullying at work settlement. Before I knew it, Vitaly was lying down on the bench and it was obviously my turn for the glove. I whacked him on the shoulders and the back. I dragged the birch twigs with my gloved hand wondering if I could get a Siberian to wince with pain. No chance. And I wondered if I should be doing the groan.

The Russian mayor of Salym, the European Field Manager, deepest western Siberia, a darkened room that was hotter than hell, stark naked apart from the pointy white felt hat that should have had "twat" written on it, birch leaf stuck on each nostril, getting and giving a good beating with superheated twigs, ripping skin off with the prostate glove – weird, but just another day at the office.

Did I do the groan? You bet.

CHAPTER TWO

Christmas, Skis and Dodger

I WAS 25 and working offshore on a UK oil production platform, and I loved it. I spent 6 months hiding from the guy whose job it was to tell me I was posted to The Sultanate of Oman. I gave the radio room operator on the platform a nod and a wink, to tell anyone looking for me that I was on night shift and couldn't be disturbed. I didn't answer the house phone for weeks at a time when I was off shift. I went off grid.

It was 1990, no mobiles and Sadam was about to invade Kuwait. They finally found me. Told me I was relocating to the Middle East, and I got on the plane to Oman on 4 August. This was 2 days after Sadam marched into Kuwait City. I didn't have a clue how close Oman was to Kuwait, so we just went. We assumed no one would be shooting and packed a flak jacket in case they were.

On the same plane to Muscat, were about a hundred young, fit, British men, with short haircuts. They didn't seem to need visas or passports, all with Twickenham Touring Club baggage tags – more about them later.

It was hot. The plane door opened, and it was like opening the oven door to get in with the turkey. Oman was a spectacular country – generally closed to foreigners, with a genuinely wise and benign ruler who spent the oil money to everyone's advantage. We would be in Muscat for 5 years – my daughter would be born there; I'd survive a plane crash landing and we would adopt Dodger.

Pristine coastline with abundant marine life, a big Indian/Pakistani/Filipino workforce, 10,000-foot mountains, rolling sand dunes and 1,000 kilometers of gravel plain. An Islamic country, welcoming to foreign residents, 4 hours' drive from Dubai, wrestling with the dilemma of opening up to foreigners or staying closed to preserve its rich culture.

The house took a bit of getting used to. We had lizards. We didn't have those in Yorkshire growing up or in Aberdeen at University. And they hadn't made it to Brent Charlie. So, the first one that scuttled up the living room wall, got my attention. I decided it was like having mice, so I needed to get it out of the house. Lizards are pretty fast, but I'm quite determined. Half an hour later, in a game of tag, with me coming second, I'd reduced the furniture to sticks and the lizard was still at large, not even panting – it stayed like that for the next five years.

... it rained half an hour a year, so why bother.

It was almost Xmas, and it rained. The house had a corrugated iron roof. The roof leaked, and the bedroom suspended ceiling came down on the bedroom floor. It was like heavy, wet, sandy cardboard – a real soggy mess. I tried to get the roof fixed, but everyone pointed out to me that it rained half an hour a year, so why bother. They did put the ceiling up again though. Briefly.

The solar water heater on the roof packed in. A crew came

round to fix it. First thing they did was drain the hot water tank onto the roof. The roof leaked. So the new bedroom ceiling, a week old, was on the bedroom floor again, in a soggy mess. No point fixing the ceiling. More determined - this time I did arrange to get the roof fixed.

It was a bungalow, so with the suspended ceiling on the floor, you could lie in bed looking at cables and the underneath of the corrugated iron roof. Xmas day, having a little lie in, there was a bit of noise on the roof – I blamed the lizard. Then one of the corrugated iron roof sheets moved, and blue sky and sun appeared. A little Indian bloke stuck his head where the iron sheet used to be, and said they'd come to fix the roof. Oh good – Merry Christmas - I must remember to be less determined more often.

We got to know the Indian foreman quite well over the years. He had the world's worst toupee. It looked like it was made of coarse nylon, and it moved independently of his head. He often shook his head to say 'no', and when he did the toupee stayed still. No idea what would have happened if he'd ever nodded a 'yes'. Being super observant, I didn't notice for the first two years.

A container of personal effects arrived from the UK. I went to the quayside for the Royal Oman Police to take everything out box by box, for the customs inspection. We were doing well until a set of snow skis appeared – demonstrating what they were for, to an Omani policeman took some skill – all on a quayside with an audience. Fortunately, he found the ski boots as well – my lucky day – so I got to demonstrate those as well. A couple of years later, and I sold the ski boots as matching plant pots – it was for a bet. Then out came a set

... the policeman got weighed ... then without his boots or gun ...

of digital scales – still on the quayside, I got weighed, to demonstrate them. Then the policeman got weighed, then without his boots, then without his boots or gun, then his boss. It was a 40-foot container and a very long afternoon.

The coast and mountains provided a playground for adventure sport lovers. My wife came back from a morning climbing with her chum and said, 'there was a litter of puppies at the bottom of the crag this morning'. Surprised she didn't have one in her pocket already; it was only a matter of time before we were driving out to the crag just to make sure they were alright. By that time, the bitch and two of the puppies had been killed by foxes, and the remaining two puppies were sorry looking specimens with limps, coughs and not much future. One second after arriving, we adopted one, and the chum, the other. And Dodger entered our lives and would be with us for 12 years or so. The dog was free, his airfares and breath, were unbelievable.

THE DOG'S BOLLOCKS, NO BRASS AND A BREW

The wild dogs in Oman are all the same shape, size and temperament. They are generally sand coloured, the size of a Cocker Spaniel, but built like a whippet. Designed to survive in the summer heat, the harsh environment and eat scraps from hunting or foraging. Dodger was different – he was white with black spots. Obviously at the back of the queue when camouflage was handed out, partial to a delivery naan bread from the local Indian restaurant and he curled up on our bed to sleep.

Brilliant with human beings, but a snarling bundle of teeth on the end of a lead if he spotted anything on four legs. There were no kennels, or vets, or "pick up your dog shit" signs in Oman.

When we went on vacation, we had to get a house sitter. He was really a dog sitter. Dodger test drove a few dog sitters, but loved Chris. Chris was in Oman as the bag pipe maker and repairer, for the Omani army pipe band. Yes really. He was also a mad keen runner. We would come back from leave; Dodger would be deaf from days listening to Flower of Scotland on whatever Chris was repairing and he'd have been out doing 10-mile runs. Every day. As fit as a bag pipe makers dog.

As fit as a bagpipe maker's dog.

He was happy with Chris, but he'd let us know he was miffed at being left, by shredding a casual settee. Sometimes two. Given the option, Dodger would naff off to go run with the wild dogs, so at a certain point I had to do a Donald. Build a fence.

Just after the Gulf land war broke out, I was at work and driving down a desert road in South Oman, quite close to the Yemeni border. Oman was always worried that the Yemeni's would use the distraction of the Gulf War to take back the oil rich Dhofar region of Oman. I saw in the distance a couple of LandRovers either side of the dirt road. As I got a bit closer there were a few pale blokes and a couple of machine gun emplacements. I came to a stop next to them. A London voice shouted out, "Do you want a brew mate?". I'd found some more of the Twickenham Touring Club.

During the land war, the British Air Force were running air refueling tankers out of Muscat airport. The crews did 24 hours on, 24 hours off, living at the 5-star Intercon hotel. Didn't take long before "Muscat Intercon – Best Foxhole in The Middle East" t-shirts appeared. The US had an Air Force contingent there, but the Omani's made them live in tents, through the summer, at the end of the runway. Reasonable in my view.

Building Dodger's fence, there was no B and Q – there wasn't even a B. Never mind a Q. I needed a visit to Ruwi High Street. Ruwi was a magical place of a hundred little workshops, where treasure could be found, grown men could be made to cry and you could have anything made. As long as you accepted it would be a bit shit. I got a mast foot for my German wind-surfer made there, and a spare. It was a very complex shape, I gave the guy the original, he produced the perfect piece of nylon bar, which he found by feel in a pile of junk, and he copied the mast foot on his pre-war (first) lathe. Cost about 2 quid. It didn't quite fit, and every once in a while, the sail would go sailing without the board. But then the lathe guy was almost blind, so what could I expect.

... you could have anything made. As long as you accepted it would be a bit shit.

If you went to Ruwi for some stuff, you had to know what you wanted, but also predict they wouldn't have it, so have a plan B, plan C and Plan D. You also needed to have all day. So off I went, I needed timber and 50, 1 and ½ inch 8-gauge screws. I went to the shop that had everything if only they could find it, which they never could. Arkwright's in Open All Hours – just bigger and hotter – and only 3 and a half candles.

"I'd like 50, 1 and ½ inch, 8-gauge screws."

"Certainly, sir".

Half an hour later after much rummaging in the back, "we don't have 1 and ½ inch screws".

"I'll have 1 and ⅜ inch then please".

"Certainly, sir".

Another 20 minutes goes by and the same slow pace rummaging. "we don't have 1 and ⅜ inch screws".

"Could you tell me what you do have".

"Certainly, sir".

15 minutes goes by, "we have 1 and ¼ screws".

"Great I'll have 50 of those please".

"But not in 8-gauge, Sir".

"10 gauge will do".

"I will go and check, Sir".

I'd been there 2 lifetimes by now and the guy in the shop had had a birthday. "We have 10 gauge". Excellent. "But do you want brass or steel?"

Unprepared for this question, with an unexpected option in front of me, I froze. If I say "brass", is he going to come back after a rummage and say he hasn't got any, in which case I will have no alternative but to slap him quite hard and be deported.

"I'll have brass". Risky. True enough, 20 minutes later, "We haven't got any brass".

So, Dodgers fence had steel screws. His next experience would have had him climbing the fence if he'd known.

One daughter had been born by this time, and the little blond bombshell with boundless energy, had become Dodger's partner in crime. He loved her to bits and guarded her like she was, well, a puppy. And she may as well have been, so close were those two. She had one of those baby gymnasium things, where you lie on your back, reach up and spin, or pull, or slap little shapes, with as much force as you possibly can, whilst getting extreme pleasure from the noises of the rattles, bells and squeaks.

One afternoon, from the living room, Dodger howled in terrible agony. Mistaking him for the baby gymnasium, and being just the right height, blondie had reached up, got hold of his bollocks in one hand, was using all the squeezing power she'd been training for, wasn't letting go but was loving the noise that toy was making. Dodger was standing on three legs, tears running down his face and giving it a full open mouth Bloodhound howl. Well you would.

... desperate to lick where his bollocks had been ...

Obviously bomb proof with humans, especially short, cute ones. But years later, in an effort to stop him attacking anything on four legs, we finished the job my daughter started, and had him castrated. At the vet, this time. He'd be about ten, and his breath and tooth decay were making me gag, so in the same general anesthetic, he had some teeth out. Poor guy, woozy from the anesthetic, he was desperate to lick where his bollocks had been, but his mouth was too sore. And no one was doing it for him. Sometimes you're the dog, sometimes you're the tree.

After 5 years in the desert of Oman, I was posted to a remote location in an old French colony in West Africa. We broke the news to Dodger, got him a guide book to West Africa and he started French lessons - while we saw just how much money we could possibly spend, to get a wild dog from a Middle Eastern desert to a remote West African rainforest.

CHAPTER THREE

The Rainforest, Mba and the Greve

IT WAS PROBABLY 10 years too early to give me this job. That was my thought as I flew into the oilfield in Gabon, arriving as the new Field Manager. It was a fly in, fly out oil field – the dense rainforest meant there were no roads connecting to the rest of the country. It was the main revenue earner for the country, well over a thousand people were in my new field, and it was as remote as it gets. I crossed the equator at least 4 times a day when I went from the living camp to the office.

Gabon is an old French colony with a mix of African and French heritage, culture, tradition and language. Thousands of kilometers of untouched tropical rainforest, multiple tribal groups and permanently pissed off elephants. Forest elephants.

Every tribe had its own language, but French was the single common communication. I'd passed 'O' level French, with a Yorkshire accent, no idea how – and right now that didn't seem quite enough to start being the boss of 1500 people. I was 33.

Language wasn't the only thing the French had left. There was democracy, but with an African flavour. The President had been President for 30 years. There were 2-hour lunch breaks, a French Foreign Legionnaire base on the coast nearby and perfect croissants and baguettes every morning. A selection of red wine at every lunch and dinner. And a unionized approach to everything – think French air traffic controllers on an Easter weekend.

Mba, my new PA welcomed his new boss with a shrug of the shoulders, and a page of typed A4. "La jeunesse d'ici a vous inviter d'assister au greve le Samedi matin". The young people in the field were inviting me to a "greve" on Saturday morning … No idea what a "greve" was though – must find out – sounded nice – sports event, presentation of awards, great Gabonese croissant bake off, wine tasting – nice welcome, obviously a thriving and healthy community spirit.

Think French air traffic controllers on Bank Holiday Easter weekend.

It was only Tuesday, and the week got busy, Saturday approached and so far, Mba had done a lot of dismissive shrugging, that other French legacy, but said nothing. Friday, he spoke – actual words - and asked if I'd read the note. "Yes", happy to come to the "greve" – looking forward to it. Another shrug.

No google translate in '97, so Friday night, getting the dictionary out to check on a "greve" – I needed to know what kind of congratulatory speech I was going to have to make.

"Greve – noun – strike". They were all going on strike. Tomorrow – in about 12 hours. I couldn't even pretend they'd taken me by surprise. Great start to a new job.

It continued like this for the next 3 years – every day, I got out of bed, knowing that there would be a bizarre event, just no idea what it was going to be.

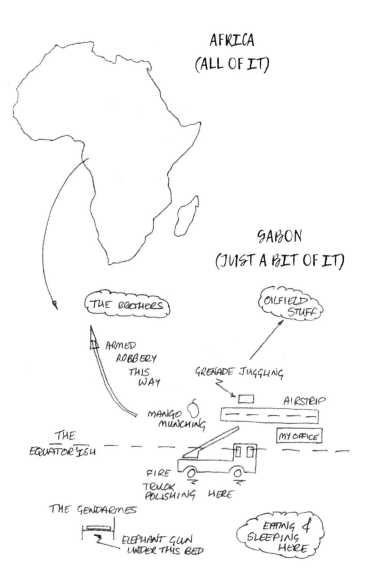

AFRICA
(ALL OF IT)

GABON
(JUST A BIT OF IT)

THE BROTHERS

OILFIELD STUFF

ARMED
ROBBERY
THIS
WAY

GRENADE JUGGLING

AIRSTRIP

MANGO
MUNCHING

MY OFFICE

THE
EQUATOR'ISH

FIRE
TRUCK
POLISHING HERE

THE GENDARMES

ELEPHANT GUN
UNDER THIS BED

EATING &
SLEEPING
HERE

Talking of beds. I started off doing week on/off in the field, with my family living at the coast – in the family residential area an hour's flight away. Later, we moved back to Europe, and I did 28 days on in Gabon, 28 days off in the UK.

I lived in a camp in the field – being the boss, I had a whole half a portacabin. By way of total contrast, in my half portacabin in the jungle, I had a Louis XIV reproduction dressing table, armoire and king size bad. With all that kit in there, there wasn't room to stand on the floor. Apart from that it was great.

I found myself sleeping in the President's bed.

Legend had it, that when the President came to open the field, a large house had to be built on a small hill overlooking the field, for the remote chance that the plane flying him in for an hour or so, had a problem and he was stuck overnight. Perfect croissants and the half litre of wine, wouldn't have been enough to make him feel at home, so the specially built house had to be furnished to a high standard. Hence the Louis XIV gear. Years later, the special house was our training centre and clinic, and I found myself sleeping in the President's bed. As t'were.

Still in the President's bed, I was woken up by my pager. That was never good news – todays bizarre event was early.

One of the permanently pissed off elephants, had attacked a LandRover and in the general mess about that followed, had got a thread protector on its trunk. Some pipes that you use in the oilfield screw together, and until you screw them together, you protect the end of the pipe with a plastic sleeve. The sleeves were made of hard plastic – about the same consistency as a car dashboard. This pipe had been about 4 inches in diameter. So, the thread protector was about 4 inches diameter too. And by coincidence this pissed off elephant's trunk was unfortunately about 4 inches too. So, the plastic – deliberately fluorescent pink, so you can see it better – had fitted like a glove.

Happy with his days' work – one bust LandRover and one terrified driver later - the elephant ran off into the forest, complete with his new fluorescent nose gear, to go and consider what to do with the rest of its day. It was only 6am.

A few days later, and the elephant was spotted again – he was pretty distinctive – the only elephant on the block with custom jewellery. There were a few digital photos being shared around, and speculation that his trunk, below the pink nose ring, was going green. Genuine worry for the elephant and genuine worry that he was now really pissed off. Lots of discussion with the clever people, but no smart ideas how to help the elephant. I was still 33 but ageing rapidly.

A few weeks later, and there was video of Punky. He'd been given a name – just to tug at the emotions a bit more. Speculation that he was more pissed off. It was the same with the bears in Siberia, when you get to that chapter – when you've got an animal problem, everyone's an expert. But eventually you realise that it's only the bear, or in this case, Punky, who really knows what he's going to do next. And he wasn't telling.

I woke up in a cold sweat from a nightmare - a vision of Punky with jewellery, feet in the air, in the Louis XIV king size bed, on one side of me. The President, stuck in the field for the night, on the other side, interrogating me why one of his loyal voters was dressed like that. Time for a holiday.

Punky was being seen pretty much every day now.

In later years we had an elephant attack an early morning croissant delivery van. None of the experts saw that coming. The driver had seen a particularly big and aggressive elephant in front of him and had put the van in reverse. At high speed, and in a panic, he ran off the road into a deep drainage ditch, turned the van over, escaped through the driver's window, just as the elephant stuck his tusk through the van's roof. Later, I caught the end of a weird conversation about whether it was an animal attack incident, or a road traffic accident. And if it was an animal attack incident was the root cause human behaviour or excessively tasty croissants. I needed a lie down and a holiday.

For Punky, we'd found a wildlife specialist in Botswana. For an unbelievable fee he would come and wave a magic wand and make everything ok. We believed him. We flew him in the next day. He got off the plane – khaki shorts, khaki waistcoat and panama hat turned up at one side. Daktari or Eric Morecombe, I couldn't decide. He had a pouch with darts and tranquiliser, and a dart gun. Punky must have been watching. He wasn't seen for the entire week Daktari stayed in the field.

I thought I was running an oilfield

Before he left, he told us what we would need for success next time.

1. Himself with shorts and lucky hat.
2. A team of 20 trackers to search through pre-arranged sectors of jungle, at night.
3. The fire crew and fire truck on standby – I'll explain why. 4. Someone to coordinate over the radio. 5. A technique to get the plastic cylinder off Punky's trunk and 6. Someone to do it – I'll explain why. 7. A couple of weeks of intense effort.

And I thought I was running an oilfield.

Fire crew – a team of 5, with a French fire chief. They normally manned the state-of-the-art fire truck. They were on standby when we landed planes at the airfield. That happened three times a week. The other 165 hours a week, they ate. Or slept. Or polished the fire truck.

A tranquilised elephant is unlikely to conveniently nod off in front of you. It's likely to run off into the forest. Might go 10 metres or 200 metres before the tranquiliser takes effect. While it's tranquilised, the elephant can't control body temperature. I took great delight in giving the fire crew a job. For 2 weeks they'd be eating less, sleeping less and no polishing. They'd be chasing a hopefully sleepy Punky round the forest with buckets of water to keep him cool. I'd never seen so much shrugging.

If we ever got Eric Morecombe and Punky on opposite ends of a dart gun, we wouldn't have all night to get that tough plastic off. Frank was a French Canadian, who lived in Calgary. He had a dead pan sense of humour, lots of initiative and liked a mission. I liked Frank.

He took some thread protectors on leave. He picked up his toolbox. He walked into Calgary zoo, which is an elephant specialist zoo. Who knew? He said, can I go practice on your elephants. And he did.

In case you ever need to know - an elephant's trunk is not round – there's a flat side facing its mouth. Heavy duty tin snips can fit in the gap between nose ring and back of trunk. Job done. Nearly. Just needed Punky to show up.

I sat on the roof of my LandRover, watching Punky munching mangoes, as the plane came into land. We had Daktari and his 20 elves on board. The fire crew had found some buckets but still lacked a sense of humour. Frank had his torch and toolbox. What could possibly go wrong. Right on touchdown, Punky waved goodbye and went into the jungle, as I waved hello to Daktari.

Eric talked us all through the plan again. And then landed the bombshell. Of course, when darted, Punky could turn and charge the team, in which case regrettably, shrug, we'd have to use the elephant gun. I checked my memory banks for any prior mention of "elephant gun". I checked my pockets in case I had one and didn't know. "What fucking elephant gun?"

As last minute changes to plan go, this one took the croissant

There was world class synchronized shrugging, and a general sense of 'your problem, Chris'. We needed an elephant gun and someone to use it if need be. An elephant gun has a bore of about an inch, and has more to do with artillery than a rifle. They are relics of the worst of the colonial habits. The recoil must be enormous and it would be so much better if you had someone who knew what they were doing. As last-minute changes to plan go, this one took the croissant. But the place never failed to surprise.

About three weeks before, there'd been a bizarre event. 50km away, there was a small work camp in the forest in the grounds of a really nice rambling old colonial-type house. The house belonged to two French brothers who'd been there many years longer than was good for them. They ran a forestry company. Their workers lived in the small work camp. There were no roads connecting their house to anywhere you'd want to go. We let them use our flights whenever they wanted to go somewhere. Which was whenever they wanted to go anywhere really.

A few weeks before, a couple of their workers had held the brothers at gunpoint, whilst they stole the payroll. Then the two workers marched off into the forest with the loot. But no map.

We had a couple of gendarmes in the field. They lived in a separate little camp. I never did know why they were in the field; they were just there. It was easier not to ask. They ate a lot as well. And slept. Not with the fire crew. They didn't have anything to polish, but they wandered around looking important with their pistols. Word got to us about the armed robbery a couple of days after it happened. The gendarmes had something to do for the first time in years, and they headed off to see the brothers. On the way back they narrowly avoided running over the two exhausted armed robbers. They'd got lost in the forest and were lucky to find a road. But unlucky to find the gendarmes. In handcuffs, we put them – the robbers, not the gendarmes – onto one of our flights. Job done and time to go back to sleep for another year.

Fabrice was my head of security and an ex-French Foreign Legionnaire. At the mention of elephant gun, Fabrice piped up that he just happened to have one. I was of course no longer surprised – of course you do Fabrice. The armed robbers had used an elephant gun to hold up the brothers. The gendarmes had taken it from them. But had forgotten to submit it as evidence. In fact, it was still under their bed. Any suggestion that they were planning to sell it was entirely untrue.

So now we had an elephant gun and three bullets. Fabrice was missing the thumb and first finger on his left hand and had a knife wound scar running across his forehead and one cheek. He said he knew how to operate the elephant gun and I believed him. He went to extract it, or buy it, or bully it, from the gendarmes. I was confident.

A few years before, the Presidential elections had got violent. So, for the recent presidential elections, a few people had been identified as potential targets. One of them was me. Fabrice had been my nominated bodyguard. He was 1.70m tall, 1.70m wide and 1.70m thick. The main security job was to search the bags of people getting on the plane, to stop them nicking things. So how one bloke thought he'd be able to smuggle a grenade he'd found, onto the plane, I've no idea. That had been a couple of months before. The sight of Fabrice juggling a grenade into my office with his one and a half hands was fresh in my mind.

I considered staying under my desk for the next few days.

Fabrice came back with the elephant gun. Ten minutes later, there was a BOOM from the office next to mine. From my new vantage point of under my desk, I saw Fabrice's boots come into my office. He realised where I was and bent down. He was bent over double and I was under my desk. We had a conversation like that, without either of us acknowledging it was just a little odd. He sheepishly explained that we now had only two bullets. He'd used one trying the elephant gun for size out of the next office window. There was no shrugging, I was less confident and glad the next elections were a very long way off. I considered staying under my desk for the next few days.

This handpicked team of talented and highly skilled professionals, with me as their expert leader, spent the next two weeks scouring the jungle. We managed not to lose anyone in the rainforest at night - result. We didn't shoot anyone – a surprising result. Nobody got attacked by a charging elephant – result. The fire crew didn't get their buckets wet - mmmmm. Frank's toolbox was unopened - bugger. Daktari's shorts remained pristine. The only people tranquilised were the gendarmes. And we didn't see Punky.

CHAPTER FOUR

Nuns, Nuts and Narcosis

I'VE ALWAYS BEEN keen on sport. But I've never been hampered by having any talent. Swimming as a kid. Rugby and running as a teenager. Beach lifeguard in my student vacations. Squash and triathlon in my twenties.

In Oman, I would come home to the capital city Muscat for my week off. I would put all my big boys' toys in the back of my open top jeep. Every morning, I'd look at the sea from the bedroom balcony. If the water was flat like melted chocolate, then it was a water-skiing day. If there were white caps, it was windsurfing. Somewhere in between then my diving gear would get a workout.

In Gabon there was little to do. A hundred expatriates living in a clearing in the rainforest – mostly families – we all knew each other. All the benefits of a small and isolated community. And all the drawbacks. There was a swimming pool – so a bunch of us started Tuesday evening swim training. There were dirt roads with no traffic, so groups got together to mountain bike. And there were endless forest and beach trails to run – so running groups formed. And one squash court. Golf was popular – amongst the elderly and self-important.

You could organize anything – a Punch and Judy show in Chinese - and it would be a sellout. 'Cos there was nothing to do. Clearly, the place needed a triathlon.

Golf was popular — amongst the elderly and self — important.

This is how quiet Gabon was. Elephants love banana trees – not the bananas, but the leaves. We had a banana tree less than a metre from the bedroom window where my 3-year-old slept. Regularly, on a morning, we'd find the banana tree had been trashed through the night. But the elephants never woke my daughter doing it. So, if by chance, at night, someone spotted an elephant amongst the houses, they'd ring you to tell you. Within minutes there'd be a group of people on your patio to watch the elephants. You're more likely to smell them than see them or hear them at night – a factoid that may come in handy one day.

The evening before my daughters third birthday, we were icing a cake in the kitchen. It was a Dalmation cake – a detail you don't really need. It was a Friday - this is a detail to bear in mind. We got a phone call to say there were elephants in our garden. We put out the lights and went onto the patio to watch them. There were four elephant silhouettes. They must have walked past the kitchen window earlier. Within half an hour, we had 20 people on our patio. It was 9pm on a Friday evening. They were all in their pyjamas.

There was a squash court in Gabon – four walls with a roof. No air conditioning – I had some seriously sweaty battles with my squash partner of choice, and oldest friend – Jim Ruby – more about him later. We'd just had a long rally in the front left corner, and as we walked away a lizard fell from one of the roof beams. It scuttled off across the floor. Not an unusual event. You just opened the court door and ushered them out with your racket.

A few moments after the lizard, a snake hit the floor – must have been on the same beam as the lizard, trying to eat him – no wonder he fell off. The snake didn't scuttle off though – it just looked hungry and cross. It was a critical point in the game, and we were both ultra-competitive. Apparently – and it's not in the rules - you can't usher a snake with a squash racket. The snake bit the racket, got it's fangs caught around the racket strings and couldn't let go. It seemed like a problem, but problem solved actually. You just chuck racket and attached snake out of the court, get spare racket, finish the game and worry about snake later. I believe I won. And the snake lost.

In Siberia, we ran outside right through one winter. Minus 26 was the record for doing our 6km circuit. No lycra – full cold weather gear – big arctic boots - scarf over mouth and nose – ski goggles over eyes – a bit iffy as we were always running on ice in the dark. We tried cross country skiing at lunchtime, since it wasn't totally dark then - until someone woke a bear. The joke was that you didn't have to ski faster than the bear, just faster than the other bloke you were skiing with. Since all the Russians were shit hot cross-country skiers, and I wasn't, being the boss, and the slowest, I had to ban cross country skiing. Obvious really.

... you don't have to ski faster than the bear, just faster than the bloke you are skiing with ...

Manila was different. A big grid locked

Asian city. There was everything to do but getting to it was just about impossible. When the tail end of a typhoon came through, we had friends who left home at 5pm to go to a restaurant for dinner. Stuck in traffic and flooding they couldn't escape, they got to the restaurant at midnight. The staff hadn't bothered to go home – they knew it was pointless trying. Our friends had dinner – it was quite good apparently. Left at 3am. Got home about 8. Literally, a night out.

Getting back from an overseas trip on a Friday, it could take six hours to get home from the airport, less than 10km away. Two hours in the car to get to a game of squash or a swim was not unusual. So, you thought twice about going anywhere and usually didn't bother. Then we heard about diving in Coron Bay. Which was about 500km away.

I've been back to Manila many times since – fifteen years or so after I lived there. The airport is as modern as they get, the roads and traffic are sorted. Even arriving on the day President Duterte was elected – an expected flashpoint – the general sense of lawlessness that had pervaded Manila, had gone. A modern, functioning city full of the most hospitable and cheerful people in my world. I was glad to see it.

But in 2000 or so, getting to Coron Bay was a challenge.

Coron Bay is in Busuanga Island. At that time only accessible by a two-day, one night, ferry trip. Now you can fly in and it's on the backpacker trail. Filipino ferries sink on a regular basis. This was a worry. But there's a whole Japanese fleet from WWII sunk in Coron Bay which was just too tempting. We'd heard of a British guy in Busuanga who may have had dive cylinders, and may have had a compressor, and may have known where the wrecks were. You could get him for a half hour, every few days, by satellite phone. Maybe. You could make out one word in three. So, could he. It was a bit loose.

We thought we'd arranged for 4 of us to be on the ferry arriving in Busuanga, to do some diving, on someone's boat, and stay somewhere, for some days. You go with the flow.

We asked a Filipino lady to go and buy us ferry tickets, gave her money and off she went to the ticket office. We didn't hear from her for an afternoon. Finally, she appeared – there'd been an armed robbery in the area of the ticket office, so she'd had to lie low in another shop for a few hours. You really did think twice about going anywhere in Manila. She'd got tickets – couldn't get one of the only four, four-man cabins on the ferry. So, we had tickets called "top deck bunk, no AC". She'd also opted for "no food". In her words, "you wouldn't like it".

So, four Europeans turned up at the ferry dock in Manila, with around a thousand Filipino's, a mountain of dive gear, a lot of excitement, several cool boxes of food and several crates of beer. It was like a scene from Liverpool docks as the first settlers left for the New World. We found our bunks. We were in different areas of the top deck. It was literally the top deck. We didn't need AC – air conditioning – we would have the breeze when the ferry was moving. The only shelter was a tarpaulin strung over the top deck. The bunks were two high,

... like Dunkirk without the shooting

with four sets of bunks pushed together – little communities of eight - probably 240 bunks in total. Next to the 4 cabins these were the best bunks. It was like being at Dunkirk without the shooting.

Bob was at the front of the boat – his seven bunk mates were nuns – he settled in for a night cuddled up at the righteous end of the boat. Neil was diagonally opposite me on a top bunk nicely under the tarpaulin. Next to me was a man and his dog. The dog preferred my bunk. His owner seemed happy with that arrangement. John was in the top bunk in the last row at the back of the boat. It was above the engines. They weren't making the kind of noise that sings you to sleep. The tarpaulin didn't quite stretch that far. Rain was forecast. And inevitable. Unlucky.

It got to teatime, as we steamed out of Manila Bay. We thought we'd all go sit somewhere together and open a cool box. And a case of beer. We sat against the ship's bulkhead next to the door that obviously led into the ship's bridge and crew accommodation. The door screamed, "No Entry" in every language. We were happy there. The crew came and went. They smiled and nodded on the way past.

Of course, it started to rain. The door still screamed, "No Entry". So, we ignored that and moved inside the door, leaning against the corridor wall. We knew we shouldn't be there, but it was the only place that wasn't bedlam, or wet. The crew came and went. And smiled and nodded. We smiled and nodded. And tried to be invisible. We were behind the bridge and forward of the officer's quarters. An older Filipino officer stopped to talk to us, and we got ready to be turfed out. Instead, he asked us if we wanted to see the bridge. So, we did. Turned out to be the captain. He'd been running container ships into Hull for a couple of lifetimes. He knew all the pubs in Hull. Great bloke.

It was a dark and stormy night outside. It was dark and pretty stormy inside. We took up residence on the bridge. You could see the lights of a hundred fishing boats around us. And couldn't see the other hundred that didn't have lights, but were for sure there. Officers came and went, and we got comfortable, quietly having several more beers and happy to be cool and dry. Around midnight we realized we were completely alone on the bridge. And the mystery of why Filipino ferries sink, was solved.

Bob went to bed with the nuns.

Bob went to bed with the nuns. As it were. I negotiated for a bit of bunk space with the dog. And John went and got deaf and wet. Seemed fair.

The next afternoon we anchored at Busuanga Island. It was a scene from the British colonies in the 1800s. The ferry was surrounded by dozens of Bankas – local built small wooden boats, with bamboo outriggers. The ferry and most of the passengers were going on to other islands – many bankas were cooking food and selling it to passengers. Think extreme Deliveroo. Some bankas were replenishing the ferry. Think Tesco. Some bankas were picking up passengers and transferring them to the island. Uber.

And there was us. Amazingly, Chris, the British bloke who'd had half a broken conversation with me by satellite phone, was there with a banka. The ferry swarmed with crew from the bankas manhandling stuff between banka and ferry. Dive gear and cool boxes disappeared. Bob said a fond farewell to his nuns. The dog stretched out on my bunk, glad to see the back of me. And John dripped his way down the ladder, straight onto the banka.

Chris, a Filipino boat crew, a dive air compressor, 40 or so dive cylinders – he'd rounded up every steel bottle on the island that would hold air - a mountain of gear and the four of us. We were going another hour and half by banka to another island, doing a dive on the way.

The dive was … incredible. A blind entry at 36m into the engine room of Maru something or other. Phenomenal visibility. Then thirty metres through the tube where the drive shaft had been before it had been salvaged, exiting through the stern gland. No other divers around. According to Chris almost no diving going on. Just too difficult to get to Busuanga. Any divers reading will know that diving doesn't get any more adventurous than this – no recompression or medical facilities for hundreds of miles, diving at the limits of recreational air diving, in unmarked wreck entries. Every dive for three days was just as good. And just as deserted. It was the experience of a lifetime.

I've been back since. You can now fly twice a day to Busuanga Island. There are hotels and hostels and more than 25 dive operators. Many of them cheap and shit. Every wreck has a couple of dive boats moored up. They wouldn't let most divers go anywhere near the good diving – they are just not good enough. And I saw three incidents in just a couple of days. I was truly saddened.

Ferry trip survived, and the one dive for that day done, it was a happy bunch that sat on the banka having a beer. We drew up to "The End of The World Restaurant". First, an island appeared on the horizon, then a wooden jetty and then a wooden hut restaurant. You wouldn't want to rely on passing trade. We were staying on Aussie's Island – I can't remember his name, but he was the Aussie stereotype. So I'll call him Aussie. At that time, virtually every rural hotel, restaurant or

"The End Of The World Restaurant"

43

tourist business in The Philippines, was run by a European, Australasian or North American man, and his Filipino wife. The men were in their fifties. They'd called in for a weekend on their way home from a bit of war in Vietnam or Korea, and never left. The woman was the legal owner, did all the work and knew who and when to pay off. It seemed to work.

Aussie was no exception and his long-suffering wife, Virginie, was also no exception. The food was unbelievably good. The beer was cold. The water was warm. All was good with the world. Rats ran up and down the beam of the wooden hut restaurant – but it didn't seem to matter. Aussie and Virginie had bought the island, built the jetty, built the restaurant and built the hut where they lived. They'd planted cashew nuts. The crop had been good. The bottom had dropped out of the cashew nut market. Who knew there was ever a thriving cashew nut market? Aussie had made nut liqueur with the crop. Then he'd set out to drink it, with a passion. As a business plan it wasn't perfect.

Around ten o'clock, in what was obviously a well-practiced manoeuvre, Virginie dragged a comatose Aussie off to bed – literally hand gripping shirt collar, and heels dragging in the sand. She pointed vaguely over the hill to where we'd be sleeping.

I've been back to that island too. I knew that Aussie and Virginie were rapidly going bust and were going to Australia. The island had been sold and a resort built. The resort had been destroyed in a 2010 typhoon and not rebuilt. Kind of a ghost town that should never have been there, on a paradise island. I was truly saddened. Again.

Over the hill, in the dark, we found a three-sided wooden

hut. Wooden floor, tin roof. There was a raised bit in one corner – Bob had that, as a mark of respect, because he was the boss. We dossed on the floor. We woke a few hours later to the most beautiful sunrise, over the bluest sea, sharing a contented silence with the very best of friends.

THE SILVERBACK, THE MEDIC AND STUPID QUESTIONS

You made your own fun in Gabon. What every tropical rainforest village needs is a triathlon. Swim, bike, run. I organized it as a team triathlon to get as many people involved as possible. In each team, one-person swimming because they could, one person cycling because they had a bike and one person running because they couldn't swim and didn't have a bike.

Over the next few weeks, teams looked for people and people looked for teams. There was a genuine buzz around the place. Routes were measured and trialled and kept secret and leaked. The pool got busy. Trophies were bought. Tyres were pumped up as high as you could – then put in freezers to get them cold – then pumped up some more. For a non-competitive, social event – it was cutthroat.

54 fine athletes in prime condition, in 18 teams. Every family had someone competing, timekeeping, marshalling or otherwise involved. Everyone had an opinion. The company put on a special flight to bring teams down for the weekend from the main office. Secret training was spotted. Transfer fees were being negotiated. People think Kona is the home of triathlon – well that year it was Gabon.

I was out one morning trying a cycle route on my mountain

bike. We had dirt roads through the forest. I was battering along one of them, when I saw in the distance someone come out of the forest on the right and cross the road. Strange to see anyone. I kept cycling fast, head down. After another hundred metres, I saw they'd sat down on the pipes running along the roadside. Unusual. As I got close, I saw the silver back gorilla sitting on the pipes was watching me approach intently. I had a moment of panic and a momentary

... silver back gorilla ....
watching me,
watching him,
watching me ....

dilemma – screech to a stop and turn around – or really go for it and hope the gorilla was more surprised than me. As I flew past, I had the image of the silver back in the corner of my eye, watching me, watching him, watching me. Not a regular hazard for triathlon – mmmmmm.

So, I thought I'd better have some medical cover. I arranged for a medic to be on standby for the event. The resident doctor was too busy - he was cycling for one of the teams. I considered using the lagoon for the swim – allegedly no crocodiles – but I had seen a very suspicious shape pass in front of me whilst water skiing. So, in the interests of safety, I opted for the pool.

Early on the morning of the triathlon, I got up and cycled down to the pool to set out lane markers. We didn't have real lane ropes, so it was going to be red and white hazard tape, stretched down the pool, weighted at either end with my dive weights. It was only 6am and I hadn't put my lenses in. I knew the pool well – I'd done many kilometers looking at the bottom of it. Which is why I was surprised when I saw an odd shape at the bottom of the pool. I couldn't make out what it was. But it didn't look good.

It was at the deep end. Which was very deep. I got in, swam to the deep end. I dived down and surfaced a minute later. With a dead cat. The side of the pool was extremely high compared to the water surface. I couldn't get this large, stiff and soaking wet cat out of the pool. I did my best lifeguard tow towards the shallow end with the moggy. Then I stood on the side wondering what to do. A moral dilemma. I'd been at the pool the night before and it hadn't had a resident dead cat. The cat had been in less than 12 hours. Was there a health hazard and I had to cancel the triathlon.? Or did I keep quiet and risk half the company getting sick?

I had the on-call medic for a reason. I called him. I was driven mostly by the fact that someone would have seen me with the cat, and would dob me in – to be honest. He was a French only speaker with no sense of humour. He had less sense of humour at 6am on a Saturday morning. And even less sense of humour with the Brit on the phone, struggling to explain a problem about a cat and a swimming pool. He told me to come round to the room he lived in – it was only a one minute walk away. For reasons best known to me, I took the cat with me. As my witness, I guess. I knocked on Mr. Grumpy's door. He opened it. He looked at me, he looked at the cat. He said there was nothing he could do for the cat. Not even one smile.

For reasons best known to me, I took the cat ...

We had a conversation about swimming pools. His professional opinion, driven mainly by the fact he wanted to go back to bed, was that there was no health hazard. I'd passed the buck, and didn't have to bin the triathlon, so I was relieved. And I felt a little foolish for asking. So, I went back to the pool with my tail between my legs, and the cat's tail in my hand. I was running out of time and didn't know what to do with the cat. I chucked it over a hedge and hoped no one spotted it. Or owned it.

Among other duties, I was doing the pre-swim briefing for the swimmers. In an uncharacteristic fit of honesty and full disclosure – I can't now believe I was that stupid – in the pre-swim briefing, I mentioned that morning's unfortunate incident of the cat and the pool. And the professional opinion of Dozey the medic. I was passing the buck further really - thought someone might bail. But no one batted an eyelid.

Except one lady swimmer. Who asked, "was it in my lane?".

CHAPTER FIVE

Morphing, Neftyaniks and Invoices

AMONG THE MANY things I loved about Russia, and remote Siberia in particular, were the traditions. Given that Stalin had ethnically cleansed on a regular basis, forcibly moved people around the Union of Republics and created more hardship than we have ever experienced in the West – old traditions and Russian culture were alive and kicking.

The first day at school for 7-year-old kids was an event celebrated in a unique and touching way. All parents, local dignitaries, school staff, existing pupils and new pupils line up around the quadrangle. I was usually there as a local dignitary – I was embarrassed to be treated like that but loved every minute of immersing in the culture. Children often started nursery at between 2 and 3, and we had built and equipped a nursery for 200 children – it was the enabler for mothers to get back to work. At 7 years of age, children would move to their senior school, and stay there until 17. They would have specialist teachers, but they would keep the same form teacher from 7 to 17. Close bonds were formed – the form teacher was talked about as the third parent.

All the pupils would be dressed in traditional costume - in the West, no teenager would be seen dead dressed like that, but the Russian teenagers were proud to keep traditions alive. Someone would walk around the quadrangle ringing a hand bell. We would present all the new children with little backpacks, tablets of paper and pencil cases full of stuff they would need. At a certain point, the oldest and biggest pupil – probably 17, would lift the youngest and smallest new pupil – possibly not quite 7, onto his shoulder and walk around the quadrangle welcoming the new pupils. Parents were crying, teachers not much different and we onlookers were genuinely touched.

Perhaps inner-city schools in deprived areas of Russia and Europe are similar: bullying rife, teachers more like security guards and expulsion the tool of choice. But that hadn't reached Siberia.

Every profession had a professional day, where members of that profession were celebrated, received congratulations and presents. Perhaps even certificates of merit if they had made significant achievement. There was a secretary's day, a driver's day, an accountant's day and there was "Den Neftyanik" – oilman's day. It's in October. I was privileged to go to Khanty-Mansysk on more than a few Oilman's Days to collect awards on behalf of my company and my team.

There is a man's day at the end of February, where women pay homage in a genuine way, to the strengths and culture that men bring. There was no embarrassment – it was a day of genuine appreciation. Of course, all Russian women will tell you, that they are just making an investment for women's day. Women's day is a week later in early March – it gives men long enough to prepare, but doesn't allow them long enough to forget.

And women's day was a day where men pay genuine respect to the women they value – wives, daughters, mothers, colleagues, bosses, staff - all women. It was a heartwarming, feel good and genuine day that everyone looked forward to and everyone enjoyed. This was in total contrast to International Women's Day – held on the same day throughout the world – but which has morphed into, and feels like, "We hate men day". Same starting point, different result. I know which one I prefer.

It wasn't all good. We had strict speed limits within the field. We alcohol tested everyone when they came into the field. We had radar guns and several road patrols out daily. Around significant holidays – New Year, Orthodox Christmas in early January, Easter, National Day, Oilman's Day – we would have speeders desperate to leave the field, and the drunks trying to get back in. Absolutely predictable, and nothing we did changed that risk taking culture.

Birthdays were treated seriously – especially jubilee birthdays – those that are a multiple of 5. I was pretty ruthless at making sure the people in my field did not negatively affect Salym village. Once in the field, you stayed. There was no nipping in for a drink on a Saturday night. I stopped staff going to the village church on a Sunday. I stopped people going to the lake in summer to cool off. I stopped staff in winter going to jump in the traditional cut out in the ice, for the cold-water purge.

There was reason. A village of 3000 people, with an oilfield of 6000 workers 50km away – most of them from out of region - is a recipe for social impact. Negative social impact. There had been a social impact assessment before the project had started, and we understood the risks. I'd read the Social Impact Assessment, from cover to cover, or at least the translation into English. There were many issues contained in it. But the sentence that I never recovered from was, "… the prostitutes of Salym are undeservedly inexpensive …". The issues this raised in my head, were many and varied – "who wrote that?", "how did they know?", "had they actually been to Salym ?". Years later, I met the author. It was a translation error. Or more likely a translator with a sense of humour.

Nevertheless, the risks of thousands of migrant workers, thirsty, with trucks and cranes and money, loose in an untouched village, were real. We spent a lot of effort making sure we had only a positive impact.

The roads were diabolical – Salym wasn't big enough to have a shop but it did have a hospital. The hospital was there to service the conveyor belt of highway accident victims. Around big holidays, lots of people travelled long distances, on dodgy roads, in even dodgier cars, after the dodgiest of Vodkas. In winter it got worse because the roads turned into skating rinks.

All the effort went into not getting caught.

Quite quickly, the guys in the field saw my writing on the wall. Russia is a rule-based society, with a punishment system to match. However, it was customary to ignore the rules. Despite being heavily punished if you were caught. Put up a no smoking sign, and it became a magnet for smokers. So, all the effort went into not getting caught. We were going to set key rules, and strangely, follow them. So quite quickly, my staff saw that 28 days in the field meant exactly that.

Of course, the principal qualification in Russia is a PhD in intrigue and subterfuge. So we had to have some subtle negotiation first, along with some traditional psychological games.

My 41st birthday was coming, and by then we had swelled to about 60 people in the field. I was told that we would be celebrating my birthday and I was to be in the canteen at 7pm. No problem with that – that's what we usually did for people's birthdays – nothing like a special meal to make the day different for everyone. Food gets so important in remote camp locations.

As I walked over to the canteen, I saw there were two buses. They were already full of 59 out of the 60. Engines running. I was called over. Not much option but to get on, but with a bit of trepidation as to what I was walking into.

We left behind a security guard as what seemed like the sole caretaker of the field, as the buses headed towards the village. They'd converted a village hall into a birthday venue. My fiftty-nine crammed in, along with some local businessman, the mayor of course, a couple of teachers from the schools, a priest from the church, the Imam from the mosque and me. Speeches were had, catering had been arranged, kids from the schools did some singing. And I was humbled. But also knew my arm was being twisted. From then on, how could I not allow anyone from the field to use any excuse, at any time, to leave the field.

I knew that in the coming days, the invoices would appear, for me to authorize for my birthday party in the village. What a dilemma this was creating in my head. But worse was to come. We were obliged to have a fire chief in the field, paid for by me, but appointed by the fire authority. He didn't yet have anyone or anything to be chief of. There was a fireman's professional day as well. He was a lovely bloke, always smiling, but I'd already realized that Georgi shouldn't be allowed anywhere near a fire. He'd obviously never been anywhere near one before. I doubted he was going to celebrate a fireman's day in my field.

We got on the coaches back to the field. As I got on, the organizer of my surprise birthday bash, gave me a knowing smile which screamed at me, "gotcha – you can never turn down anyone who wants to go out of the field now". Master of subterfuge and chief pusher of boundaries. In truth, they became one of the most valuable people in the field. But we needed this little negotiation first.

Master of subterfuge and chief pusher of boundaries.

We hadn't finished. As we headed down the main highway towards the turn off for the field, we took a left turn. There were no amenities in Salym, but there was a lot of open ground, and there was a lot of forest. We'd cunningly avoided all the open ground when we turned into the only fuel filling station in town. It was surrounded by forest. My birthday is in July. When the forest was tinder dry. And forest fire was a constant threat. We all got off the buses, and I braced myself for whatever was happening next.

Georgi appeared. Smiling as always. He'd been given the job of rounding off my birthday celebrations. With a firework display. My smiling fire chief had chosen to set off the fireworks – dodgy ones no doubt – from the forecourt of the fuel station. Two bus loads of people, crammed between the pumps and the kiosk and the air compressor. The fireworks would be going off above tinder dry forest, on the edge of the village. I hoped I was going to wake up and it was all a bad dream. But the first rockets went off and I didn't wake. It was mercifully short.

We hadn't wiped out the entire staff in a road accident on

the highway. We didn't set light to anyone. Or the fuel station. Or the forest. Or anything. We didn't destroy the village. And Georgi smiled blissfully throughout at a job well done. There were tough conversations needed and I didn't know where to start.

MEDALS, ACCENTS AND FULL OF SHIT

Few days are as important in Russia as "Den Veterani" – Veteran's Day. In Salym, a village of three thousand, there were 38 veterans. They were veterans of the Great War, the war in Afghanistan and the war in Chechnya. This was extended to the wives of veterans if their husbands had died in the conflict, or since the conflict. In the early 2000s, the veterans of the Great War were in their 80s.

Russia values it's veterans in a way that we have forgotten in the West, and in a way that is only just emerging again in the UK. Russians are fervently patriotic, and unashamedly supportive of their heroes. In the days before Veterans Day, you would see veterans in full military regalia, with medals polished and head held high, travelling by plane to Moscow. They are looked after in the capital, and in remote villages, and afforded genuine respect and kindness. I am an ardent supporter of this kind of respect for real role models.

With this as the backdrop, I was excited when Vitaly Yurovich invited me to take part in the Veteran's Day celebrations in the village. I did my research and got trusted colleagues to tell me what to expect. My Russian was fairly good by then, so I elected to go without interpreter. Suit and tie. Polished shoes. Wreath to lay. Speech to make. Hands to shake.

I was chatting with Gina. She was one of the village police chiefs. She'd been good to us on quite a few occasions in the early days, when she could have made life hard. I'll tell you more about her later.

There were well coordinated marches by bands from the schools. Marches by youth groups. Representatives from the regional government were there. Marches by the police, the village fire service. Readings by church priests. Local dignitaries and busines leaders – that was me – laid wreaths at the village monument. We made speeches. It was a hot day and a long morning. It was a bit much for one or two of the older veterans, and by lunchtime, the ambulance had been to give oxygen and fluids. Twice I think.

... by lunchtime, the ambulance had been ...

Nevertheless, everyone made it to lunch at the Circle Culturel – the main village hall. The 38 veterans plus about fifteen dignitaries. The veterans were traditionally given cash grants – Salym was a relatively poor village, so the grants were small – but were given and received in the very best spirit and with the very best motives. As lunch progressed, toasts started, and vodka flowed.

I was sitting with Svetlana, the head teacher at school number one. The schools have numbers, not names. I'd done many presentations at the school. When I couldn't speak Russian, I would speak in English and my interpreter would then say the same thing in Russian. When I could speak a little Russian, I'd write a speech in English, get my interpreter to translate it into Russian, and coach me through the words I didn't know. Russian with a Yorkshire accent was apparently hard to understand, so they were probably more in need of a translation than ever. Some of the kids at school were studying English. When my Russian got passable, I would speak, uncoached in Yorkshire Russian, and get my interpreter to translate into English – the guys studying English liked this. When my Russian got good, I'd swap between sentences in English and Russian. It gave my interpreter a nervous breakdown but gave everyone else a good laugh. When I finally left Salym, the pupils at school number one made a lengthy presentation to me – they did it in pairs – one spoke in Russian, and the other parodied me and my interpreter, by translating it into English. The whole school was in on the joke and I collapsed laughing. I swear they'd been practicing a Yorkshire accent.

Back at Veteran's Day lunch. In a small village, everyone knew everyone else, and everyone else's business. The local business leaders made presentations to the veterans based on their needs. A new cooker, a television, train tickets to go and see family – things they really needed. It had been a long and emotional day for the older veterans.

Russia's ability to consume Vodka is legendary – you'll read more about that later too. Russia's ability to consume Vodka is not only legendary. It's also not diminished by age. By 2pm the ambulance had been again. And again. The 38 veterans were down to about 30.

Undeterred, lunch and toasts continued. Most of the toasts were brief, expressed thanks, recalled compatriots lost and memories kept. They were all self-effacing.

Except, at a certain point, one of the Great War veterans leant on his stick and got to his feet with difficulty. He began to reminisce about his Great War service in the Red Army air force and the air battles he had survived as a fighter pilot. I was aware of a few eyes rolling, and not only from alcohol. But I was concentrating hard on keeping up with the Russian language. A couple of minutes later, he recalled close shaves and the terror of his time in submarines. There was a general bit of restiveness now. I sensed a bit of whispered ridicule. A couple of minutes later another tall tale started. And there was some muttering on one of the other tables.

... I've known you for 68 years ... and you are still full of shit.

On the opposite side of the room, another elderly veteran got up. I could see Vitaly Yurovich's face go a little pale. The toaster was now recounting experience with the Red Army infantry besieged at Stalingrad. In a big loud voice, the elderly gent on the other side of the room, shouted, "Ivan Ivanovich ... I've known you for 68 years ... and you are still full of shit!"

Ivan Ivanovich stopped talking. Red with rage, but with unbelievable speed for a man in his eighties, he set off across the room waving his stick in the air, ready to dish out a bit of Stalingrad to his accuser. I was half a sentence behind the conversation. But I saw Vitaly Yurovich launch himself between the two of them, saying, "Don't hit him again, it'll really spoil the day".

Someone took Ivan Ivanovich home. And the survivors got back to lunch. Without missing a beat, and without a trace of embarrassment or humour, just stating a fact, Vitaly Yurovich leant over to me and said. "It's a village tradition".

CHAPTER SIX

The Mamba, The Badger and Dinner

IN REMOTE PLACES, the chance of wild animal encounter is higher than your average Yorkshire High Street. Animals have been some of the toughest dilemmas and given the most amusement. Without exception, everyone wants to do the right thing for wildlife. Without exception, the wildlife doesn't understand that.

We avoided driving around at night in remote places, likes deserts, because it was hazardous for the humans. But sometimes there was no choice. The desert of Oman was no exception. But there were camels everywhere. They looked wild. Until you had a vehicle accident with one. Then the owner stepped forward instantly from behind the nearest bush, to claim compensation for his highly valuable pregnant racing camel. Camels have this big heavy body on top of long spindly legs. You can't see the body in car headlights, it's too high up. You can't see the legs until you are close, because they are thin and blend in with the background – in fact, you can't see them until it's too late. We always went to unbelievable lengths to keep people and wildlife separate. Always looked for what more we could do. But I wonder what happened to the guy who wanted to fit wild camels with reflective kneecaps.

For the first couple of years, we didn't have bear encounters in Siberia. Then the regional government got serious about stopping poaching, and the bear population rocketed. At the same time, we brought more people into the field, started working more areas. So, the number of human to bear interactions grew. Everyone genuinely wanted to protect the bears. And the lengths we went to were extreme. Ask me about the story of Clyde, and you'll see what I mean.

A decade earlier, I came back to Gabon for my 28-day shift. I got off the plane and with my bag over my shoulder I walked the 300m to my office. My back to back – Jim – the guy I shared the job with, would be happy to see me. Not because he was actually happy to see me. But it meant he was going home for a month. As I walked into the office to meet him, there was a scream, and I found him standing on the desk. After 28 days of relentless stress, and sleep deprivation it was normal to be a bit highly strung. But this was weird even for Jim. As I'd walked in, he'd opened the desk drawer to find the stapler, and instead found a Black Mamba napping.

... a Black Mamba napping.

Not really an animal story, but I can't resist. In Siberia, my boss came to visit from Moscow. Garry is a gentleman, well liked and highly respected. He must have a PhD in 'doing the right thing'. He religiously did the 2 days of arduous travel each way every month. He was always a welcome sight. This day, as he sat down on the sofa in my office, there was something different. I couldn't figure out what. We talked about him moving to a new apartment the previous week, whilst I tried to figure out what it was. After a while he stopped talking, and said, "you're looking at my hair?" Then I got it.

Being a man who liked to nurture every Rouble, he cut his own hair with electric clippers. Being a man of a certain age, he was thinning a little on top, though still with a full set of medium length black hair. Being a man of Gaelic origin, he was so white skinned, he was blue. As Billy Connolly would have said. In a rush to look beautiful for his trip to Siberia, he'd been searching through his post move cardboard boxes for his clippers. Couldn't spot them and got frustrated. At a late moment he found them, plugged them in and trimmed away. He'd forgotten the guard and had taken a stripe from front to back down the middle of his blue scalp. A reverse Mohican if you like.

Undeterred, he'd gone for some slightly less vigorous trimming everywhere else to disguise his stripe. And he'd gone for a bold comb over. Then he'd gone for his flight. It was a decent disguise job, but as he finished telling me, all I could say was, "I've had bosses do strange things before, but you're the only one to disguise himself as a badger".

It was meant with respect, compassion and empathy. No really. The oilfield is a brutal place, but all our attempts to get his photograph that visit were avoided. Nevertheless, we got his passport photo from somewhere. Found a friend of a friend of a friend in a graphic design place. And managed to get a very authentic blue'ish stripe airbrushed in. Copies were made and framed. As is traditional in Russia, there is a copy of the boss's photo up in many offices – Mr. Putin the President being on many a wall. In our case joined by Garry the Badger. I think Garry appreciated the thought.

If you find a nerve, of course you are duty bound to give it a good twang at every opportunity.

THE WORLD (JUST THE IMPORTANT BITS)

THE BADGER

YORKSHIRE

TWICKENHAM TOURING CLUB

REFLECTIVE KNEE CAPS

AFRICA (THERE'S LOTS OF IT)

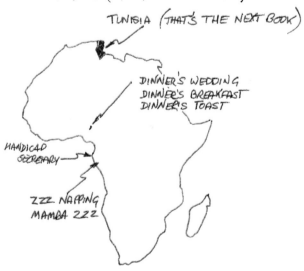

TUNISIA (THAT'S THE NEXT BOOK)

DINNER'S WEDDING
DINNER'S BREAKFAST
DINNER'S TOAST

HANDICAP SECRETARY

ZZZ NAPPING MAMBA ZZZ

In West Africa, I'd been invited to a wedding, along with another Brit. Weddings are not my thing, but it was lovely to be invited, so off we went. It was a two-hour drive, on a potholed road – up hill and down dale, or whatever is the West African equivalent. We had a normal saloon car. Fortunately, we had a good driver, Chibiko. The security situation in this bit of West Africa could be challenging even then and a 2-hour cross country drive was not to be taken lightly.

We'd researched the customs and traditions for a wedding in that area, for that tribal group. We knew it would be an all-day event. We got there about ten. The groom's family were sitting around one big table, the bride's family around another. The bride's family occasionally gave the groom's family a new expectation as dowry for the bride. The groom's family would then go off and find it, buy it, borrow it, make it – you get the idea. The guests do most of the drinking, dancing, encouraging and bedlam creating. So, sacks of rice, crates of drink, washing machines and gold jewellery appeared - as did various animals. By 4 in the afternoon, to the inexpert eye, there hadn't been much marrying done, but there was a mountain of stuff. We had to go – we couldn't risk the drive back in the dark. We felt bad, but people had been coming and going all day, so it seemed alright.

As is traditional, when guests leave, the bride and groom give them a present from the present mountain. A bit arse about face for us Europeans. We got a chicken. I'm terrified of birds, so I could have been more thrilled. We gave the bride and groom genuine thanks for a great experience. And for the chicken. The dilemma of where to put the chicken in the car got solved. It went in the boot. For two hours, every time we went over a pothole, the chicken would run from one side of the boot to the other squawking. The chicken got a name – animals always do - courtesy of Chibiko. It was christened "Dinner". I felt there was a clue to the bird's future in this name. We got back to the house that I shared with my colleague and wondered what to do about Dinner. The security situation was such that every window and door had bars up outside to stop intruders. So, Dinner had a long piece of blue string round one foot, with the other end tied to a bar outside my bedroom window.

There was a clue to the bird's future in it's name.

This was a mistake because he liked squawking. But by 6am, the squawking had stopped, and I nodded off for an extra ten minutes. When I got up, the blue string was empty. Chibiko was full. And Dinner was breakfast.

But blue string would feature heavily in Gabon.

SANGO, JAMES HERRIOT AND SMALL CIRCLES

As well as the fire crew and the gendarmes, we had a medical team in the field. And we had a medical centre – in that house that was built for the President – remember?

The medic was Dominique. He was from Reunion – so not really French. And never known to shrug. We needed a medic. Anywhere you have a thousand people, someone is poorly. In the tropics, poorly can be very, very poorly. We were an oilfield too, so Dominique did occupational health. He did medical aid to local villagers. Most importantly, in the event of an accident, Dominique and his boys were the trauma care team. You hoped the medical team were bored. And some of the time they obliged.

Dominique himself, was an active guy and very ethically driven – always looking for the opportunity to do good. He passed his free time birdwatching and, like a small village, everyone knew that.

I came into the field for this particular 28-day shift. Jim wasn't on the desk this time, and from the chair, he said to me in passing that Dominique had an injured bird up at the clinic. Not in itself unusual. Jim hadn't seen it, and neither of us recognized the species from the description in French. In general, I would stop by the clinic early in a 28-day trip to see if we had any medical issues I needed to know about. Communicable disease – Hepatitis wasn't a stranger, stress related illness, shortage of medicine – whatever. And I liked Dominique. I made a mental note to go see him. And the bird.

Animals needing help were not an unknown event. A baby elephant had appeared earlier that year. After a couple of days, it was clear he'd got separated from his mother somehow. He was the size of a St Bernard dog, probably a few weeks old. On the phone to Calgary – we had connections to the zoo there - we got instructions on hand-rearing a baby elephant – milk, sugar, a funnel and a feeding schedule. You may thank me for that tidbit of knowledge if the need arises. And surprisingly, Sango thrived. They always get names. And he became very tame.

Whenever we had a lost, abandoned or sick animal, we would ultimately hand them over to the brothers who ran the forestry company. The ones that got robbed that time. We would help them in other ways. Quid pro quo. They had a menagerie of random semi-tame animals, that had been brought to them by various people, up at their house in the forest. After a couple of weeks, Sango went up to the foresters. If we wanted to escape the work grind for a couple of hours on a Sunday, we'd take a drive over to the foresters. You'd get out of the car and be greeted by Sango. He'd come running over and stick his front feet on your shoulders. No problem with a St. Bernard. By the time he was six months and the size of a donkey, this was an issue.

... he was six months and the size of a donkey ...

Between the foresters and ourselves, we spent weeks arranging a small aircraft, making a crate and agreeing for Sango to go to a wildlife park in central Gabon – a famous and genuinely well respected one. And one weekend we made it happen. I like to think Sango is telling his new elephant mates about how he used to guzzle milk and sugar and stick his front feet on my shoulders.

Dominique. A few days went by, and I hadn't got as far as the clinic. Someone mentioned that Dominique was now feeding an injured bird up at the clinic. The way they used their hands told me it was a big bird. Sometimes I felt I should know what was going on in my field. Mental note - must go see Dominique.

A few more days went by, and I'd got engrossed in urgent issues. Only 300m to the clinic but I hadn't made it there yet. Now the story was that Dominique was treating the injured bird with antibiotics. It was Alexandria – another name. And she was described as a Stork.

The next bulletin on Alexandria, was that Dominique was operating on her injured wing that morning. I needed to know what Jimmy La Herriot was up to. But the door traffic had been relentless, and Alexandria hadn't got to the top of the list yet.

The next day, at lunchtime, I was alone in the office block. My office was the first on the left as you came in. The outer office door was a swing door with a distinctive squeak, and a door closer that made it slam and the whole building shudder. I was sitting at my desk. I heard the door squeak open. I heard it slam shut. Shudder. Deep in my brain, I registered that I wasn't hearing the usual footsteps. My peripheral vision hadn't picked up anyone walking past my open office door. These two things, and my subconscious, made me look up.

Nothing. Then at about chest height a yellow beak. Then a white bird's head and a long thin neck, looked at me round the edge of the door. I went cold. It had been a frantic time, but I was seeing things and I'd only been there a week. I really did *... a big white body, on top of gangly legs ...* need to go see the medic. For myself. Then a big white body, on top of gangly legs, one of which had some blue string attached, came round the door. It hadn't even knocked.

Followed by Dominique.

At least I was ok. It was a bit odd to have a big white bird report to my office for work. But at least it made some sense. Dominique said he'd heard I'd been interested in Alexandria's well-being, so he'd brought her to meet the Field Manager. He introduced us in very formal French and picked Alexandria up. With her immense body in the crook of his arm, her head was about the same height as ours. Alexandria wasn't fazed, and I'd recovered a bit by now. As we spoke to each other she did the tennis umpire thing – moved her head from side to side to look at who was speaking. And did that constantly.

She was doing very well apparently, antibiotics taking effect, eating well, though part of one wing had had to be amputated because of the injury. She'd been brought in by a local villager. He'd caught her in a trap meant for something else. Dominique extended the uninjured wing, with Alexandria looking at it as he did – bigger than any wing I'd been close to. With Alexandria watching, he extended the injured wing – there wasn't that much to extend. I asked him if she'd be able to fly. After some deep thought, Dominique gave his considered professional opinion. Perhaps in small circles. I believe I saw Alexandria nod.

The office block door squeaked open and slammed shut. Shudder. In walked one of the engineers. The three of us – Dominique, Alexandria and I looked up in unison. "Alright Alexandria?", he said. Without even breaking stride. Clearly, I was alone in needing therapy. Or they were all in a plot to convince me I'd lost it.

What happened to Alexandria? She went to the forestry brothers too.

CHAPTER SEVEN

Contractors, Rottweilers and Murder

I DIDN'T HAVE anything to do with police or security as a teenager. I hated getting into trouble. One look at a blue light and I'd have gone bright red, held my wrists out for the cuffs and pleaded guilty to any crime you suggested. That was my starting point for police and security services.

All that changed when I went to Gabon. Among other things, I had a security team of 25 Congolese guards. Congolese because the Gabonese didn't trust the Gabonese. And Fabrice, the odd shaped ex-French Foreign Legionnaire, with half a hand, that you met before, to run them.

Security issues, when it gets beyond simple theft, can be prolonged events. So, when a security incident starts, you know you can be in for a long job. Danny was a Teessider. He ran the construction crew. About 400 people, who lived together in a separate camp a few kilometers away. The construction crew were made up of 50 or so Thai welders – highly skilled and irreplaceable. And 350 Gabonese mechanics, electricians, labourers, crane drivers and helpers – not so skilled and often considered replaceable. Most of them were employed by one

Gabonese contractor company. Every couple of years we'd retender the construction contract and take the lowest bidder. So potentially we would have to change out the contractor, along with all the risks and hassle that included. Which is exactly what had happened.

Changing out a contractor was a risky time – the guys who weren't going to be taken on by the new contractor, would be generally unhappy, not surprisingly. The ones who had been taken on by the new contractor, could be generally unhappy – their new terms and conditions weren't always what they were expecting. It was a time of general unrest, distrust and suspicion.

We would also be trying to keep construction going, even though minds would be elsewhere. Deliberate sabotage wasn't an unknown event. Whether it was a smooth transition or not, we had hundreds of people to move out of, and into, the field, by plane – so the logistics were a challenge. And for everyone, there was the gut-wrenching uncertainty of whether it would be a smooth transition or not. Conventional wisdom is that you announce, and do, contractor change out, in as short a period as possible. We were going through exactly that process when Danny called me one morning.

In Russia, when Putin became President, he proudly stated that he would put 60,000 FSB agents back into industry. FSB is the domestic equivalent of what had at one time been the KGB. I had two FSB agents reporting to me in Siberia. They ran my security team. You knew they were with the FSB because their CVs said they were graduates of the FSB University. Not too covert so far. You also knew they were only working for you fifty percent of the time. You could learn to work with them or try and work against them. They were well connected, powerful and had incredible reach – in Russia and abroad.

My two worked month on, month off, back to back. They could not have been more different. Dimitry was tall, slim, blue eyed, blond haired, highly perceptive and highly intelligent. If anyone had told me he was a psychological warfare major, with a listening device in my office, and a truth drug in his, I would not have been surprised. We had mutual respect, real trust and we learned to work together, we understood each other's boundaries.

... a listening device in my office, and a truth drug in his ...

Sergey was the other one, and we hadn't – learnt to work together that is. Sergey was short, squat and heavily built due to hours in the gym. If anyone needed leaning on, he was probably the man for the job, and he'd probably done it already. Sergey should always have had a very big Rottweiler by his side.

It's the only time I've been given a request to buy shotguns, riot batons and stun grenades. Sergey and I had to have a bit of a conversation.

The Gabonese security team weren't overly subtle. If we had a snake problem, they were the answer. The first time I had a snake under my Louis XIV reproduction bed, where I kept the bag that I used for travelling, I called Fabrice. I wasn't sure what I was expecting – maybe some local traditional method of hypnotizing snakes into a coma and then releasing them into the bush. Maybe Fabrice would circle the snake - all of his senses on alert, and with the speed of light, grab the snake behind its head, wrestle it to the ground, skin it and eat it – that's what you expect the Foreign Legion to do, right ? They did neither. They stuck the muzzle end of a shotgun under my bed and pulled the triggers. The snake was no longer an issue, my bed was a bit less Louis XIV and I needed a new bag. Standard practice apparently.

In Siberia, we'd had an incident. In a remote place in the forest. Late in the afternoon, we had a man trapped by a large piece of equipment. The equipment had shifted in transit and trapped him by the foot. The location was about 75 kilometers along a highway, and then 10 kilometers along a forest track which was mostly swamp. The unfortunate guy was actually trapped in a river. As more information came in, he was trapped in such a way that his teammates were holding him above water. It was April in Siberia and the rivers had just unfrozen. We needed to get heavy lift equipment a long way through deep swamp areas. It would take hours. In the meantime, the man would drown unless his mates could hold him out of the freezing river until we got there. Emergency response was my job. There was no help possible from civil authorities. We were on our own. I was feeling the weight of responsibility. I'd rather have been anywhere else in all honesty.

I'd rather have been anywhere else.

Information was sparse. The trapped man worked for a contractor building a pipeline. This contractor was state sponsored and so had the monopoly for building pipelines. They were ok at building pipelines; they were not ok at anything else – like looking after their people or cooperating with me. A classic case of having no choice, tolerating them and looking forward to the day they left my field, job done. But in the meantime, they had a bloke to rescue, and I was relying on them to do that.

Trust was limited. So, I sent an English speaker, Steve, along with Sergey, to the junction between highway and forest road. Instructions were to get eyes and ears as close to the accident site as possible. It would take them a couple of hours to get there. In the meantime, I spoke with the manager at the pipeline contractor and reluctantly they admitted there was an incident, reluctantly agreed they were moving cranes and medics and reluctantly agreed to keep me informed. In Russia, knowledge is power, and power is not for sharing. Trust was now non-existent.

Back in Gabon, when Danny called me that morning, he didn't sound right. He should really have been turning up in my office for a daily meeting around that time anyway. *Today was hostage day.* What was he doing phoning ? In his best Teesside, and in a strangely formal way, he explained that he was in his office in the construction camp. And he had a small problem that was delaying his departure. A good size group of Gabonese contractors were unhappy at being flown out as part of the contractor change out. In fact, they didn't believe that the contractor would pay them what they were due. So, they weren't going to leave. In fact, there were thirty of them in Danny's small office – I could tell there was a bit of bedlam going on. And apparently one of them had a knife to Danny's throat and he was being held hostage. Every day a bizarre event, you just didn't know what it was going to be. Today was hostage day.

Steve and Sergey got to the Highway junction about midnight that night. Information from the pipeline contractor was non-existent – they just didn't feel the need to tell me what they were doing. I was more worried they were doing nothing. They had a traditional blame and punishment culture – they'd be expecting blame and punishment from me. They'd probably started blaming and punishing someone already. I was only interested in saving the man – and it was not looking good. We were worlds apart.

About one in the morning, Steve got me on the satellite phone. There were some lights coming out of the forest. A few minutes later, he let me know that there were twenty or so workers walking out of the forest – I could hear Russian voices in the background. A few minutes later and Steve said that these guys were part of the same work party. They'd had to abandon their vehicle because the track was blocked by the incident and they'd walked ten kilometers out through the swamp. He also said that the foreman was a few minutes behind them. A few minutes more, and Steve said Sergey had spotted the foreman and was going over to talk to him. I could hear Sergey talking – even for Sergey, it sounded more like shouting. A few moments later and Steve told me that the foreman – blame and punishment looming, and despite Sergey's bulk - didn't want to talk to Sergey. Now he was running away. Now, Sergey was chasing him down the track apparently. A few moments later, Sergey had caught him. A few moments later, the foreman was "talking" enthusiastically.

I have this vision of Sergey and his enormous snarling Rottweiler, in the mist of a forest night time, pulling some fingernails and dusting off an electrode set – I was only glad I hadn't bought him the shotguns - all in my name. I gave my head a shake – was I really doing this. And I wished I wasn't.

The incident went on all night. To cut a long story short,

by the next morning, the patient had been brought out of the forest. He'd been trapped for fourteen hours in the water, with his foot caught under a heavy machine, with his mates holding him out of the freezing river. He was a Siberian, so what would have killed a normal man, had bruised his foot and caused mild hypothermia. He was lucky. Sergey was chuffed with a good job done. I was relieved.

Back in Gabon, the Danny situation was a little troubling. I hadn't had a hostage situation before. Or since for that matter. Well you don't do you.

We declared an emergency – more because we didn't know what else to do than because we had a plan. There was a thick book of emergency response plans, but nothing under "K" for kidnap. Fabrice secured the area to stop anyone getting in and making it worse. We sent the medical team – Dominique without Alexandria – in case the knife at Danny's throat was actually sharp. And then wondered what to do next. I looked in my box of trained hostage negotiators and it was empty. But there is nothing excluded from the Field Manager's job description, so it was me. Another time I'd rather have been anywhere else. I was a 33-year-old engineer and I'd missed the college module on kidnap.

We spoke to the police in the nearest city – seemed like the right thing. And it made me feel better. But they weren't that interested, had no ideas and wished us luck. Bye.

I talked to the contractor CEO in the same city as the police – a plan emerged. We'd get them a hundred-seater plane – we knew how to do that bit. A few of their management, from the same tribe as the hostage takers, would fly in. As the guys who didn't trust the contractor to pay them, got on the plane, they'd be given a bag of cash they were owed at the bottom of the steps. As plans went, it left me with some moral dilemmas. And as plans went, what could possibly go wrong. But as plans went, it was the only one likely to help Danny keep both ears.

An hour later Danny was still talking, which was a good sign. The airfield supervisor called – there was a plane inbound – great! the guys with the cash. No. It was a police plane with a hundred heavily armed gendarmes coming to help. Just what we needed. I didn't feel helped. We parked the fire truck in the middle of the runway – clearing elephants from the airfield that we knew weren't there - to give us time to think.

The airfield supervisor called – there was a plane inbound – I knew, and we didn't want them. No – it was the guys with the cash. The police plane had been too short of fuel to hang around and had turned back. Result. Magically the elephants that weren't there, weren't there. And we welcomed the money plane into land. The day was tense but improving.

A queue of guys formed at the bottom of the plane steps. They got a carrier bag full of the cash they were owed. In return they got on the plane without Danny's ears. And I admit, in return, none of them got a job in my field again. And finally, in return, I got Danny back to talk Teesside another day.

Why did it always happen when Sergey was on shift? The American government and the Russian government had fallen out over something. We had a camp with all the smaller, mostly temporary, contractors, living in it. In fact, it was an open area with many small camps. One small camp housed an American owned specialist contractor. There were a dozen or so Texans living there. Bless them.

We used to get the most violent electrical storms. Russian

technical law had provided for this. There were no other amenities whatsoever, but luckily we had plenty of lightning conductors. Lattice steel towers about 20 metres high, with ladders built in. A small platform on the top. A steel spike another 5 metres high, mounted on the platform.

I got a call on my duty phone. That was rarely good news. Someone had put the Stars and Stripes at the top of a lightening conductor. Just the kind of rational thing you'd do with a bit of international tension in the air, added to some longstanding mutual distrust. The dozen or so Americans were living in the small camp surrounding this conductor. We didn't need DNA to figure this one out. A thousand or so Russians were living in the surrounding camps. Didn't the Alamo start like this.

... the Alamo started like this.

I'd have to do something before there was a murder. My Siberian field was the size of Wales. I was in Cardiff and the Stars and Stripes were in Anglesey. The manager for the contractor was a Dutch driller. Drillers are culturally conditioned to do exactly what they want – they need that kind of autonomy to do their job.

I have many Dutch friends. It is widely recognized that the Dutch are culturally conditioned to do exactly what they want. But even this driller had to admit that the Stars and Stripes might have been an error. We had a bizarre conversation about American civil liberties – but in the end I just had to tell him – "flag down now".

I wasn't altogether trusting that this subtle hint would penetrate a drillers' psyche. And if it did, that it would be relayed the length of Wales, quickly. And if it was, that an American, in the middle of a government dispute, could bring himself to lower the Stars and Stripes. But if there was a murder, no matter how much it would have been deserved, I'd have been left with the mess. So, I called Sergey. Fully aware that this would have him firing up his inner Rottweiler.

Off he went. Inner Rottweiler snarling.

Sergey heard the story with the gravity of a man who had been waiting a lifetime for something to do. Either that or he needed time to attach brain to foot. Off he went. Inner Rottweiler snarling.

I heard no more, and I got on with the business of producing oil. Producing oil was a minor hobby that I did a bit when I had time between being headmaster and judge. The next morning, as was my habit, I walked over to my office at 6am. It was mid-winter – minus twenty or so, deep snow, pitch black. I loved that time of day because there was no one else around. I was in my office chair less than 15 seconds when I became aware of Sergey behind me. Either he'd been hiding in the bushes all night waiting for me, or he had a motion detector in my office linked to his head.

He wasn't wearing camouflage paint, and he didn't have anyone's head in his hand. All surprisingly good so far. "The mission is complete". My heart sank. Sergey and a mission were probably not a good combination. "What mission Sergey ?". "The flag", as he handed over a full-size Stars and Stripes. There were no cannon holes in it, or blood stains. A sense of relief. I had a vision of Sergey, leopard crawling across the camp, 4am, in a US stronghold, Rottweiler on a short lead, shinning up the spike of the lightening conductor, combat knife in his teeth.

I must remember never, ever, to cross Sergey.

NERVES, OPPORTUNITIES AND THE SKITTERS

Security teams are not always the answer. In Egypt, companies employ as many people as possible, but as a result no one is well paid. And the lowest level of workers were paid extremely badly. There's also an opportunistic culture. As a result, anything and everything is liable to be nicked. Down to and including toilet roll. Which could be quite annoying. I wasn't the boss in Egypt – more kind of a hired specialist. So, I didn't need to solve the toilet roll theft issue – just had to watch while others did. Which was much more fun. We didn't put guards in every toilet, and search people as they left. We found a solution exactly fit for purpose.

I shared a small house, in a camp in the Western desert of Egypt, with Tim. Tim is not his real name – because he's bigger than me. Tim was another Dutch driller. I have heard it said, that the Dutch in general, and drillers all over the world, fervently believe in looking after number one. I can neither confirm, nor deny this rumour. Even though I started it. Dutch drillers can be especially tricky to work with. And even harder to live with.

Riding a bike in Holland is very popular. If you wear a helmet while riding a bike in Holland, two things occur. Everyone knows you are a foreigner, because only foreigners think helmets are necessary on a bike. And you get jeered at by passing motorists for wearing the helmet. The rumour, that the Dutch don't wear cycling helmets, because they have them naturally inbuilt, is simply not true and completely unwarranted. Even though I started that one as well.

Tim had upset lots of the resident expatriates in his drive to look after number one. I'd drawn a bit of a short straw living with him. As I've said before, there is a culture of, "if you find a nerve, you are duty bound to twang it at every opportunity". Tim had lots of nerves, and everyone gave them a good twang, as often as possible. The reaction was usually extreme. I had to live with this. But all in all, it was rewarding for everyone involved.

To manage the toilet roll theft issue, and so we could employ yet another person, someone came round with your personal toilet roll allocation on the first of the month. You had to sign for it, naturally. With ink, not poo. And then your destiny was in your own hands as it were. And Tim could have a change and look after number two.

With ink, not poo.

If you left your toilet roll on your desk and it got nicked, unlucky. If you left it in the toilet cubicle, it would be gone by the time you remembered and went back for it. The distributor wasn't overly generous – by the end of the month things could be getting tense.

Toilet roll is a great leveler. No matter how senior you were in the company, you need to poo. When you needed a poo, you unlocked your cupboard, took out your toilet roll, tucked it under your arm, and off you went down the corridor to the loo. If someone was coming to visit me in the field, from the main office in Cairo, at a certain point they'd need to borrow toilet roll. And vice versa if I went to the main office. It was an unspoken element of every business negotiation.

It wasn't uncommon for the foreigners in the field to get a dose of the 48 hour skitters every few weeks. At which point toilet roll took on a whole new importance. It was currency, like tobacco in prisons. You had to hope you'd got enough in the bank. Or lots of friends.

It must have been near the end of the month, and Tim had been poorly for a couple of days. I knew that because I shared a house with him, and he wasn't shy. Or quiet. Sitting at my desk that morning, Tim came along to see me all red faced, told me he was poorly, his substantial arse was sore, and he was out of toilet roll. Could he borrow some.

I thought what favour I wanted in return, but I couldn't ignore a man in that kind of need. And by this time, he was hopping from one foot to another, spittle forming at the corners of his mouth. But I did want to make as much mileage out of this favour as possible – he was Dutch after all. And a driller. I turned around in my chair, and with no great speed, tried to find the right key for my office cabinet. It was a big key ring, and it took me a while. Silly me, it was open all the time. I must have been having a good month, because I still had two or three untouched, pristine rolls of soft velvet. It was sitting at the front of the top shelf for all to see. I let Tim see the object of his desire. His eyes were wide open with relief. By contrast his sphincter was clenched tight shut with worry.

... eyes wide open with relief ... sphincter clenched tight shut ...

But I had an idea. And Tim had a nerve that I needed to twang. I parted those valuable and oh so soft rolls, because I remembered that at the back of the cupboard, I had something Tim deserved more. Tim had skin as thick as a rhino – but I thought I knew where to find his soft spot.

I inherited the office cupboard and contents from my

predecessor. In previous years, he must have left some unused toilet roll at the back. Remember when you were at junior school, and you got boxes of what can only be described as grease proof paper. It had specially sharpened folds and hardened edges and never absorbed anything, just kind of spread it about. These boxes of razor blades had obviously been given out in times past. But I still had a box. Seemed a shame to waste it.

Tim's eyes filled with hatred. As he tried not to let his trousers fill with something else. He'd have happily killed me. But he was already running away, box of blades in hand. He didn't even thank me.

Of course, karma is real. So, a few days later I was poorly, and travelling back to Europe through Cairo airport. Petty theft is a national issue, not just a company one. So even in the business class lounge at Cairo international, you'd have been hard pressed to find a square of tissue. Sitting in the cubicle, feeling queasy, but substantially relieved, I tried to think of what I could use. I was considering taking a shoe off and travelling with only one sock, when I remembered some paper in my hand luggage. I remembered to take the staples out of my International Driving License, but I did forget to remove my photo. And that had really sharp edges.

All I could think of was Tim. Reflecting that I'd scratched his arse, so he'd scratched mine in return.

CHAPTER EIGHT

Nuts, grass and shit

IN SOME WAYS Gabon was a treat, in some ways a challenge. We lived in a clearing in the rainforest with about a hundred other expatriate families. The beach was a couple of kilometers away. The rainforest came right down to the beach. So did the elephants.

We didn't know at the time, but when Dodger arrived, he was going to experience lots of new stuff. He would feel rain for the first time – proper Equatorial African torrential rain – the first time we put him out for a pee in the rain, you'd think it was raining acid – "what the fuck is this ?", as he looked upwards in disbelief. He stood on grass for the first time – it obviously tickled his paws. He hopped from one paw to the other like he was being stung.

And he would meet elephants for the first time. He was partial to a bit of elephant shit – the fresher the better. He would stick his nose in the air when he caught a whiff, and he was off – no matter how far away it was. And when he got there, he would have a good roll in it. Elephant shit is bright green. Dodger was white with back spots. Sometimes we'd come back from walking the dog, with a green dog. People would borrow him for the day. This green stinking thing on four legs would appear at the kitchen door as the dog borrower brought him back.

And he would meet monkeys for the first time. I used to run on the tracks through the forest. This was an oil field, so there were steel pipes that carried the oil, laid alongside the tracks. I would run, knowing the monkeys were watching me from the trees. But the first time I took Dodger with me, and ran past one particular tree, with a particularly big troop of monkeys living in it, all I could hear was "ping", "pang", "ping". Took me a while to figure out the monkeys were throwing nuts at the dog, and they were bouncing off the steel pipes.

He was partial to a bit of elephant shit.

There wasn't much to do in Gabon.

There was a lagoon, which allegedly didn't have crocodiles. And at some point someone had put a boat there to ski behind and bought some great gear that no one seemed to use – I was a keen skier, and not bad, so we dusted off all that kit and offered ourselves up as croc bait.

There was a jungle golf course, and the golf addicts were as insufferable there as they are everywhere. I'm not keen on golf or golfists, they're all too self-important for me. A jungle golf course and there was still a reserved parking space, with sign and white lines, for the handicap sec.

The lagoon backed on to the golf course, and the first tee was only a few steps from the bank – with a decent run up on a mono-ski, getting the apex of the turn just right, you could drench them just as they were getting ready to bat. It wasn't easy to teach Dodger to shit on the greens under cover of darkness, but we got there in the end. Just needed a bit of persistence.

And he would trash another couple of settees.

But first we had to get him there – he was still in Oman, living with friends, wondering where we were.

THE BOX, THE LIFT AND THE ILLEGAL

We left Oman on the cheap. Dodger left on Swiss Air. He had a couple of days in Zurich kennels, and then took the Swissair flight to Libreville, the capital of Gabon. The dog was free. His flight certainly wasn't – but Swissair was the only airline that would sell him a ticket.

They told me the cost would be based on dollars per kilo of dog. You couldn't buy a dog box in Oman, so I had to take a patience pill, and go back to Ruwi, to get one made. Swissair assured me that it didn't matter how big or heavy the dog box was, it only mattered how heavy the dog was. I believed them – they were Swiss. Dodger went on a crash diet. I did a drawing for the biggest dog box there has ever been. Two bedrooms, an open plan living room and a balcony. It had its own title deeds and stamp duty.

Dodger was staying with friends in Oman for a few weeks extra slimming, and until we got sorted in Gabon. Then he would hop on SwissAir with his Des. Res. He needed some crucial multilingual paperwork that said he was a dog or something. And after a long weekend taking in the sights of Zurich, he'd grace us with his presence in Gabon. Easy. Not.

I took him for his official weigh in at SwissAir. His month of dieting had reduced his weight by about a hundred grammes, and the cost by about 25 cents. But the different guy at Swissair, took one look at his travel mansion and said, "what's that?". I told him how happy I was that SwissAir would let Dodge travel in style for a nominal price per kilo of dog. He shook his head, told me it was price per kilo of dog plus residence. I went white and started choking, as only a Yorkshireman can, when confronted by a price rise. I was regretting the upper floor I'd added for feng shui. But SwissAir being Swiss, they accepted their error, honored the original deal, and Dodger would travel in his country house.

Swissair, bless them, researched what paperwork he needed to leave Oman, and what he needed to arrive in Gabon. There was a lot of it, in Arabic to leave Oman, in French to arrive in Gabon. All needed top translation and plenty of furious stamping by as many embassies as I could get interested. All to say that he was a dog.

When we arrived in Gabon, the first issue was that we wouldn't be living in Libreville, we would be two more one-hour flights, South. Two one-hour flights, in the company plane, which was quite small. Dodger's palace wouldn't go through the plane door. I didn't need a tape measure to know. Mmmmm.

And just the small matter that I'd have to take 2 flights to get to Libreville, stay overnight with Dodger somewhere. And then the two of us take two more one-hour flights back to where we'd be living. Mmmmmm.

Some phone calls from Gabon to Oman, "Yes, put him on SwissAir tomorrow, Monday". Which meant he'd arrive in Libreville 6 pm Wednesday.

Problems to be resolved:

Find a small dog box that would go on the two flights from

Libreville to new home,

Get myself and small empty dog box on flights from our new home, to Libreville, on Wednesday in time to meet the SwissAir flight,

Find a hotel that would have me and Dodger for Wednesday night – not common in West Africa to take your dog for a night away,

How to get myself from airport across Libreville, and back the next morning, with a dog.

Get myself, small dog box and dog on flights from Libreville, to our new home, on Thursday.

Are you keeping up?

But the biggie, as pointed out by Virginie, the SwissAir lady, on the phone from Libreville, in West African French that I just didn't understand well, was that the SwissAir flight would land at 6 pm. But customs closed at 5:30. So Dodger would have to spend the night on the tarmac in his box waiting for customs clearance the next morning. Which meant we couldn't get the flights back to our new home until Friday. And there weren't any. "Don't worry", she said, she'd fix it. I was worried.

I found a box from someone else who'd taken a Labrador from Britain to Gabon. It definitely went on the company plane. Have you ever travelled with an empty dog box – people think you've lost the plot – they go

... travelling with an imaginary dog.

talk to the dog, find an empty box, and decide you're travelling with an imaginary dog. Perhaps I had lost the plot.

I landed at the domestic airport – it was a shed really. It was guarded by an Alsatian on a chain. It became very important to me. The Alsation, not the chain. I left the small empty dog box, with my imaginary dog, in the shed, in the faint hope I'd have a real dog to put in there the next morning. I went to find Virginie at the international terminal. It was a slightly bigger shed and didn't have a guard dog. So as a result, there were thousands of people outside the terminal all wanting to carry the bags of international travelers. And I mean thousands.

Virginie said, "follow me". She was obviously not used to being disobeyed, so I did. We went the wrong way through arrivals. Past the customs guys checking suitcases, past the baggage claim belt, past passport control, past the guys who check your Yellow Fever vaccination certificate as soon as you get off the plane. We emerged onto the runway. No checks, no paperwork, just a friendly wave from Virginie and we were there. I vaguely wondered if I should be doing this, but it was well before 9/11 and I had no choice. And Virginie said it was ok, and clearly no one argued with Virginie.

She said, "sit". Not sure if she was talking to the imaginary dog, or me. So, I sat obediently. On one of those yellow steel barriers you see at the edge of the apron at airports. Virginie walked off and said, "stay". So, I did. Half an hour later, the SwissAir jumbo landed, and taxied to a standstill right in front of me. When I say right in front, I mean I had to lift my feet, like when your Mum's vacuuming, to let the nose wheel past. The engines shut down, the stairs were rolled up to the plane, passengers disembarked, the baggage guys did their thing. It was dark by this time and the lights in the plane went off. The crew shut the plane door behind them, put the key under the mat and went to the pub. The lights on the runway and in the airport went off. It was noticeably quiet. Virginie appeared, and said, "come". So, I did.

We climbed up the baggage conveyor belt thing, into the hold of SwissAir, and there in the corner of the cargo bay was a very big box, with a small dog, who was very pleased to see me. I didn't really want the massive box, because I didn't know what I was going to do with it. So, Dodger had a quick pee in the cargo bay before I could stop him. Sorry Swissair. And then dragged me down the luggage conveyor, while I dragged the box. I tried to sell it to Virginie, but she wasn't interested.

I got a luggage trolley, balanced the box on it, and balanced the dog on that. There was no one at the Yellow Fever checking station, lights were out at passport control, everyone had collected their luggage off the belt and gone home. The customs guys had long since stopped checking suitcases for the night and were in the pub with the aircrew. So, all that paperwork, translated and stamped – no one there to admire it. Me, and the illegal on the box, emerged from the terminal shed. With a shed. There were still a thousand people outside the terminal in case there was a suitcase to carry. It was the kind of bedlam you only get outside an African airport.

Me, and the illegal on the box …

You never gave anyone a suitcase to carry of course, because it would never be seen again. Which was my cunning plan. Give someone the box, march off quickly in the direction of the hotel car. I'd organized a car but forgotten to mention the extra passenger. Me and the illegal got in. The driver wasn't best chuffed. Seconds later the box appeared. Not only had it not gone away, but I had to pay the 4 guys guy who had carried it. They'd never actually given anything back to the owners before. Too big for the hotel car, the driver went to find a mate with a pickup truck. I had to pay him as well.

We got to the hotel – the only European standard'ish hotel I could find who even understood the concept of having a dog checking in, as opposed to trying to keep dogs out. We checked in. We were on the 23rd floor and Dodger had never been in a lift. And he wouldn't get in. After his box it probably wasn't big enough for him. Nothing I could do would get him in the lift. So, we did 23 sets of stairs – me, the illegal and the small overnight bag I'd brought with me.

The bag had got the essentials in it - two tins of emergency tuna to feed Dodger in case his delicate appetite couldn't face anything else, a bowl and a pair of underpants. They were for me. Dog fed, I was starting to get hungry myself, but before we could head off for the restaurant, there was a knock at the door. Two sweating porters. And a massive dog box that I unfortunately recognised. It wouldn't go in the lift either apparently, so they'd lugged it up the stairs. I tried offering money to lose it for me, but they didn't fancy lugging it back down the stairs. So that was a "no". It wouldn't go through the room door, obviously. So, we left it blocking most of the corridor. I made sure it wasn't between me and the stairs. But anyone further along the corridor was going to have a job on, getting out that night.

Couldn't get him in the lift again. We did the 23 sets of stairs down to the hotel bar. Dodger was knackered - he fell asleep under the table while I had a beer and some food and thought through the next day's sequence of issues. It was ten o'clock by this time, we had to be up at 5. I hadn't had three days flat on my back in a luxury box. It was raining cats and dogs – sorry – but Dodge must have needed a pee, so I borrowed an umbrella, and we went for a wander outside the hotel. Unbeknown to me, and not that I had any choice, but seemingly this was a hotel that rented rooms by the hour. There was a gaggle of young women outside, who all wanted to stroke Dodger and get under my umbrella. It was like the old black and white film you see of students trying to get the maximum number of people into a mini. He loved people, so in no time at all he'd made a dozen new friends and he'd settled in for the night to socialize with his new posse. Oh good, because I really, really wanted him to pee, so we could do the stairs again, and get to bed.

23 sets of stairs back up to our room. He still wouldn't do the lift. And we went to bed. His breath hadn't improved. The price of a long weekend at Zurich kennels luxury resort and spa for dogs, you'd think they'd have fixed that. It was a rough night's sleep. Not least because of all the scrabbling in the corridor – it was people climbing over the box in the corridor to get to their room. And Dodger snoring.

Up at 5, I was only going to do the stairs once, so I took the bag with empty bowl and pair of underpants with me, and we went for breakfast. We got in the hotel car I'd arranged and set off for the domestic shed. We only got 10metres, when the concierge came running after the car, followed by two blokes with the dog box. I offered money again to take it somewhere else – no joy. So, the convoy of Dodger and me in a car, followed by the chase pickup truck and dog box, turned up for the company flight.

Dodger had a go at the guard Alsatian, which was all I needed at 6am. But the guard Alsatian had a handler this morning. I offered free housing forever for the Alsatian, and the handler took the dog box off my hands. Result. I was in Gabon for 4 years, and every time I went through the domestic shed, I couldn't help but smile at the Alsatian and his luxury abode with all the airline stickers.

Then the howling started.

I retrieved the small dog box that I'd stashed away, kicked out the imaginary dog, and forced Dodger in. He wasn't keen – he wasn't impressed with his new gaff. And probably thought he was in for another three days' worth of being in a box.

I settled down on the first of the two one-hour flights. Me in a chair, Dodger in his box in the small luggage hold just in front of me and the other 20 or so passengers. Everyone was looking forward to an early morning nap, as you do when you are on an early morning flight. Then the howling started – and didn't stop for the whole flight – both flights. Full blooded head back, open jaw baying at the moon type howling, the sort you only get if someone has got your bollocks in a vice like grip.

A couple of hours later, and Dodger was in da house.

CHAPTER NINE

Detention, Burhans and Ibuprofen

I LOVE PLANES and flying, but I'm not convinced planes love me. So obviously, I had to learn to fly – just to prove a point. But if there are in fact 9 lives, I must be getting close.

Two winters offshore from Shetland is enough to cure anyone of helicopter travel. Horizontal snow, the lurching about of a helicopter, and an event that sticks in my mind; oil dripping from the cabin roof at about 1500 feet somewhere between the platform and Shetland, the co-pilot peering at it, and shrugging, I'll call that life #1. After all – I was only allowed offshore to finish my training, because it helped replace two complete shift teams that had been killed when the Chinook crashed the year before in 1986.

I was glad I'd done the offshore survival training – several times. It always included the dreaded simulated helicopter sea ditching, and then rollover, whilst still strapped in your seat. You always wore a one-piece rubber survival suit with built in boots – before you left from Sumburgh to go offshore, you'd be given a suit and you'd check over all the seals and zips yourself. I checked my suit, but I must have missed the ham sandwich that had been left - likely a few weeks before, in the right boot of the suit – not a great start to that trip.

And the joke was that the survival suit hood of the person in the seat in front was more perfectly placed than the sick bag if you felt a bit queasy. And who wouldn't – with or without the ham sandwich.

In West Africa, the water was warm, so no survival suit needed. But you did do the HUET – helicopter underwater escape training. And before the training you needed a swimming certificate.

It's not all truly offshore in West Africa. A lot of the oil production is from the river delta and swamp area. This meant either helicopters to get there, or small fast boats. Many West Africans don't swim – whether they do not learn as kids, or because the rivers and sea are treacherous, or the lack of pools, or a cultural aversion to swimming, I never really understood. Probably all those reasons. Either way, everyone using helicopters or fast boats in this part of West Africa needed a swimming certificate.

So, in the office area, there was an Olympic size pool. A contractor had been given the job of giving swimming lessons. The same contractor had been given the job of running swimming tests and issuing certificates. It took the contractor micro seconds to figure out that the more people that failed the test, the more lessons he had to give, and the more re-tests he could do. Voila - a license to print money.

Few foreigners went to the swamp locations – and you couldn't blame them - security was genuinely difficult to manage. It was also not much fun. An arduous trip just to get there, treated with suspicion when you did, shot at on a bad day, food poisoning on a good day. But I was keen to get there – so I nipped down to the pool to get the certificate.

... shot at on a bad day, food poisoning on a good day ...

94

THE WORLD (NORTHERN BITS)

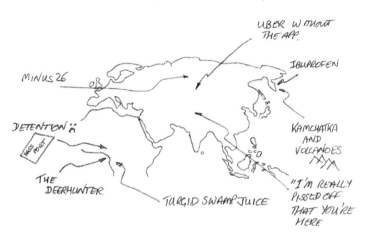

UBER WITHOUT THE APP.

IBUPROFEN

MINUS 26

DETENTION

PASS TOILET

THE DEERHUNTER

KAMCHATKA AND VOLCANOES

"I'M REALLY PISSED OFF THAT YOU'RE HERE

TURGID SWAMP JUICE

YORKSHIRE (AND OTHER BITS OF EUROPE)

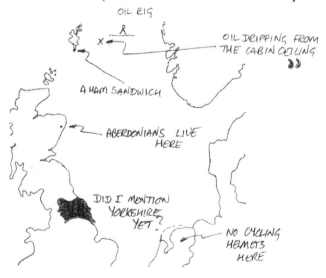

OIL RIG

OIL DRIPPING FROM THE CABIN CEILING

A HAM SANDWICH

ABERDONIANS LIVE HERE

DID I MENTION YORKSHIRE YET?

NO CYCLING HELMETS HERE

Beach lifeguard as a student, sometime triathlete and keen diver – I reckoned they could give me any test and I'd be good. Down at the pool, there were hundreds of local employees doing swimming lessons – there was a dejected air of people who knew they were never going to pass. And many more that didn't want to wait for weeks of endless lessons and repeat tests. No one was having fun. So another option had developed.

For a small consideration, a certificate could be issued without a test. It was made clear to me that I would need lessons for a few months and many tests because no one ever passed first time. I waited for someone to offer to sell me a certificate – but they didn't. I kicked up shit, so reluctantly I was given a test date, a time and a prognosis – I wouldn't pass.

You know how you smell the chlorine of a pool before you can see it? This pool was the same. Except it wasn't chlorine. I could smell stale swamp juice before I went through the gate in the surrounding wall. The water was turgid – 6 feet deep but you couldn't see the bottom - the way a pool can only get with a thousand sweaty bodies a week, and nobody chucking in chlorine. Plenty of green algae. Looking after the pool clearly didn't pay well.

On the day of my test, word got around that there was a foreigner who was doing a test, and hadn't had any lessons. There was a crowd – literally, hundreds.

The test was treated with extreme gravity. There were clipboards and stop watches everywhere. I knew that I wasn't supposed to pass. I had to jump in and tread water waiting for instructions. I did. Now swim 50m to the other end, diving under the water to go through a hoop halfway. I did. I might not survive the poisoning from the water, but the swimming was no bother. The crowd were getting into it now, with a fair bit of cheering. The examiner was pissed off – he couldn't be issuing a prize certificate without charging for lots of lessons. Or without charging. There was a "face" issue too. As the crowd got happier, he got angrier and his eyes bulged with fury.

Climb out unaided at the far end. I did. Lower myself back in, without jumping. I did. Tread water for a bit. I did. Now swim the 50m back, picking up a brick from the bottom halfway. I'd be lucky to find the bottom, let alone a brick. I asked him what stroke he'd prefer – I don't think that helped his blood pressure, but the crowd loved it. Surprisingly, I found the brick. Not sure whether to drop it again, or take it with me, I took it to the far end. I had to tread water for a minute. The crowd were now going berserk. Someone was getting the certificate they wanted, with no lessons and no cash. A minute became two, became five, became ten.

Eventually the examiner couldn't think of anything else for me to do. He gave up. Told me to get out and pick up my certificate. I did a couple more lengths just to say goodbye to my new friends. Now I was fully certified – and you needed to be – to fly to the swamp.

Years later in Russia, I was asked to go to a Northern Siberian small oilfield, operated by a small Russian operator. "Go and see what you think". I was an industrial tourist really. Aviation in Russia is hazardous, and helicopters fall out of the sky on a daily basis.

In most of the world, oil companies contract with one of the 4 or 5 international helicopter operators. They have high technical and safety standards, by anyone's measure. But in

Siberia, the prevailing preference was for cheap and short term.

If you wanted a helicopter tomorrow at 2pm, you called up a broker today and gave him coordinates. He sent something at the given time. It was like Uber without the tracking app. You had no idea what helicopter was turning up, whether the crew were any good, or sober, and they had no idea of the job. You couldn't leave a driver review either.

... like Uber without the tracking app.

I watched a helicopter come in. It was a MIL8 – the Lada of the helicopter world. Longitudinal seats, internal fuel tank, single engine, no seatbelts – virtually no instruments, so all visual flying. A hint of fog and you had to land. All the things that were unacceptable in the rest of the oil and gas world.

The job was to take a crew to a nearby rig. I watched more people get on, than there were seats. I watched freight loaded in after the passengers. A few large size gas cylinders went in next. Flammable gas, for welding. The helicopter lifted off and swung into the wind. I saw the pilot drop something in the cockpit – maybe a pen. He reached down to pick it up, lost control and the helicopter pitched and yawed violently. It was still just 6 feet off the ground. Someone ran in and connected a "long line" underneath the helicopter. The helicopter struggled to lift against the overload. At about 50 feet, the pilot took up the slack in the long line. It lifted some pipes slung on the other end of the long line and moved off in the direction of the rig. When it got to about 200 feet, the pipes – obviously not slung securely – fell off. And hit the ground just outside the residential camp. Helicopter operations Russian style. And life #2 I reckon.

Back in West Africa, I did my first trip to a swamp location. At the heliport on the way out, you had to clear immigration – the guy asked me for my "identification". The passport that I entered the country on, was away somewhere to get my work permit. But I had a second passport, so just gave him that. That was "identification" after all. The flight was uneventful. The trip was uneventful. The flight back was uneventful. After I landed, a different immigration guy asked me for my "passport". That was a different question. I gave it to him. He couldn't find my country entry stamp. I told him the story – my passport was away for a work permit – and he was looking at my second passport.

It was just after 9/11. It was illegal to have a second pass-port in that part of West Africa apparently. He asked if I was a terrorist and he wasn't smiling. I was held in custody at the heliport for the rest of the day on suspicion of being an ille-gal immigrant. I doubt anyone has ever tried to be an illegal immigrant into that area.

In Siberia, we needed to airlift a camp. The camp was built in steel containers. Ten containers for people to live in. A container with generators. One with snowmobiles. A toilet and shower container, a kitchen and canteen container and an office. There were no roads. So, we would airlift the camp. Next, we would helicopter in a tree cutting team, so we could start building a road from both ends. To lift the camp in, we needed a team of two to get to the landing area and do some preparation. This was too good an opportunity for me to miss.

Together with Tony – an ex-British marine, and Falklands veteran, who'd been an arctic warfare instructor – I took two

Burhans – Russian snowmobiles – two hours through the Siberian forest. We camped out overnight in a Millets tent in minus 26. And the next day lifted in the wood cutters' camp. We used a MIL26 – the Russian heavy lift helicopter. It's like a jumbo jet body with a massive rotor plonked on top. At the end of the day, I left Tony at the remote camp, and hitched a lift back to the main camp on the MIL26. Fantastic – that wasn't work, that was fun.

A couple of years before, I'd worked with Tony in Siberia. We needed to go inspect some Soviet era wellheads – abandoned thirty years or so earlier. The forest had long since swallowed access roads and any clearings around the wellheads. We had coordinates but any maps were approximate at best.

... the pilot landed on top of us. Literally.

We came up with a plan whereby we found the wellhead from the air, the helicopter went to the nearest clearing, hovered at about two feet, and we jumped off. The helicopter couldn't touch down because it was deep swamp - you would immediately sink up to your bollocks in swamp and be unable to move. We had rucksacks and satellite phones in case the helicopter had a problem while we were on the ground and we had to camp out. Having jumped off, up to our midriff in swamp, we would then lie on top of our rucksacks whilst the helicopter lifted off above us. The pilot would find the wellhead again and hover over it, whilst we struggled through the swamp and forest to get there. After we'd done the technical stuff, we would do the whole thing in reverse. At the pickup point, we would lie on top of our rucksacks, whilst the pilot landed on top of us. Literally.

The thinking is, that if the helicopter is a bit unstable, the safest place to be is as close to the centre of the rotors as possible. I believed it.

In some places there were fair sized saplings that could have stopped us landing – but we found that if you hovered a bit, the saplings bent over. Everywhere, the rotors were only feet from trees.

At one drop off, we jumped down, but the swamp was just too deep, so we had to radio for immediate pick up. Lying on top of rucksacks in deep swamp, as the helicopter steadied on top of us, a bear came out of the forest. There was no fear of the helicopter noise. It stood on its back legs a few metres away and gave us the "I'm really pissed off that you're here" bellow. It didn't get on the helicopter with us but was so close that it could have done.

Does that count as life #3?

A bunch of us had heard that you could heli-ski in Kamchatka. Kamchatka is a peninsula in the far east of Russia, due north of Hawaii. A long way North of Hawaii. A German mountain guide took two trips of 12 or so people each spring. He took the same pilot from Moscow every year. He was an Afghanistan veteran. And they used the only twin engine MIL8 in Kamchatka. We thought long and hard and convinced ourselves it was ok.

I spent a week in Chamonix learning to powder ski. We practiced avalanche rescue. We bought all the specialist equipment. All the gear and no idea. Skiing in Kamchatka is on volcanoes. The coast looks like Norway – long deep fjords lined by steep, high mountains. And just no people for hundreds of kilometres in any direction.

The helicopter dropped us off for one run on the tip of a volcano – we skied down into the caldera, past weird mushroom shaped formations where the steam was sculpting the ice. We skied out the other side where the caldera lip had collapsed. Each run was 40 or so minutes – straight back on the helicopter – repeat.

On another run we were dropped off high on a volcano. We watched the helicopter fly away and land at the pickup point. The pickup point was a beach next to a fjord. So, we skied from mountain top, to the beach and onto the ice of the Pacific. Wow.

I needed Ibuprofen to get out of bed.

I didn't realise, but when the weather is good, the helicopter flies and keeps on flying – from first light, until dusk. When the helicopter flies, you ski. Us Brits could all ski well. But we were with four or five Swiss, a couple of Austrians and some Germans. They'd all been born with skis on. We kept up but no more. Three days of perfect weather. I was knackered. On the third day I needed Ibuprofen to get out of bed. I was desperate for a good storm.

Ten days of heli-skiing and we went back to Moscow. I went to work in Siberia. Three weeks later, the second group of European skiers for that year were in Kamchatka. The helicopter had dropped them off, and gone to land at the pickup point. The guides and skiers had split into a fast group and a slower group. The fast group had already got back to the helicopter. As the slower group approached, they set off an avalanche. It buried the faster group and the helicopter. The two pilots, the loadmaster, the pilot's young grandson, one of the guides and 5 German skiers died.

The Russian Ministry of Emergencies mobilized helicopters and rescue teams. But by then, they were recovering bodies. By this time, I was in Moscow. En route back to Europe. But stuck in Moscow because the Icelandic volcano had erupted, and European airspace had closed. Families of the dead couldn't fly into Moscow. Bodies arrived in Moscow but couldn't be flown on to Europe. We helped discussion with the authorities as best we could. Eventually the volcano relented.

Life #4.

THE YOUTHS, A SWEDE AND ABERDEEN

A couple of years after the illegal immigrant thing, and many helicopter flights to the swamp areas later, I found myself in a swamp location again. This was an oil production station – a flowstation. It had a small camp and helipad. The flowstation was on the junction of two rivers – I never knew the names, so I'll call them river 1 and river 2. The rivers were each a mile or so wide – these were not small streams. Communities group themselves by river, rather than by village or town or district.

A few years earlier there had been a moveable drilling rig in river number one. A dispute over something had developed between the youths from river number 1, and the drilling company. Not unusual. The youths had got on board the rig, trashed it a bit and held the crew hostage for pretty much two weeks. Not an unknown event. The crew were mostly Aberdonians, and somehow remained in email contact with their Aberdeen head office through the two weeks of kidnap. That was a first. You could read their latest bulletin every day in the Aberdeen local papers. At certain points they were genuinely fearing for their lives. The rig was badly damaged by the youths. And it was more damaged by the national navy when they decided to end the siege. The rig had gone for a couple of years' worth of refit.

The national navy had decided to keep a gunboat in the vicinity of the junction of the two rivers. And they kept a crew there too. Unfortunately, they didn't give either the gunboat, or the crew, any fuel. So, the gunboat moored up on the far side of the river. A small community then grew up to sell the crew food and water. And beer. A water taxi service then developed ferrying the oil workers from the flow station across the mile-wide river for an illicit evening beer. What could possibly go wrong.

After refit, the rig had gone to start drilling in river number two. But the youths from river number one got wind of it – you can't hide a drilling rig. They obviously hadn't finished trashing the rig, so took a small armada of boats down to river number two to finish the job. From inside the flowstation fence, I heard boat engines go past one evening. And I heard the shooting start an hour or so later.

The youths from river number two weren't chuffed. Someone else was trashing a rig in river number two. Trashing things in river number two was their job. So, what else could they do - they took a small armada of boats to trash the rig as well. By this time, it was 4am and there was a fair bit of shooting. It was distant, but insistent. It was interrupting my sleep. The navy were either looking for fuel or in the pub or were sleeping better than me.

The Aberdonians from the rig weren't chuffed either. I don't know the Aberdonian for "déjà vu", but I think that's what they had. They radioed the flowstation to say they were on their way and could we flag down a passing Uber for them. We sorted a helicopter pick up, but not until first light. There were 10 Aberdonian drillers, and the helicopters were nine seaters. Overcome with bravery, I decided I wasn't hanging around either. I'd have been the only foreigner for a couple hundred miles, with bedlam brewing. So, we arranged two helicopters.

The Aberdonians arrived by boat about the same time as first light and about the same time as the first helicopter. The helipad was right next to the river. The first helicopter came in and nine of the drillers scarpered. Me and one other waited for the second helicopter. Unfortunately, the youths from river number one, or it could have been river number two, had spotted the helicopter activity. They had a taste for Aberdonians and weren't happy they were getting away. So, the shooting migrated closer to the flowstation and the helipad. The navy weren't answering the phone. Funny that.

The pilot of the second helicopter radioed to say that he didn't fancy coming into land. I couldn't imagine why not. He was going to go and hover somewhere until the boats all went away. Or until he ran low on fuel. I *... because I was shitting myself. Please. Over.* recognized the voice – it was a Swedish bloke I played squash with. They are all Sven – but he really was. Ground to air radio calls are very formal and follow a set protocol. But there are exceptions. I said to Sven that it would be really nice if he could come up with a cunning plan because I was shitting myself. Please. Over.

A few minutes later he radioed back. He'd noticed an old wooden helipad a few hundred metres or so inland from the junction of the rivers. It would be heavy going to get there through the bush. But he would hover over the old helipad so we could see what direction to go. The two of us set off. Took forever to get there. But he waited. He couldn't land – the helipad was wood and had been there 20 years. It had mostly rotted away. He hovered a foot off the ground, opened the loading door and we fell in. Like a scene from The Deerhunter.

A Yorkshireman, an Aberdonian and a Swede were in Vietnam – there's a joke in there somewhere.

And I reckon that was life #5.

CHAPTER TEN

I'm Not Much Better With Planes

WHERE I FINISHED with helicopters, I started with planes. I'd been in Malaysia for a week and was heading back to Amsterdam. I was on Malaysian Airlines MH16, flying from Kuala Lumpur to Amsterdam. It was the same night that the Russians shot down MH17. Allegedly. MH17 was going Amsterdam to Kuala Lumpur. The flights usually crossed paths somewhere over India.

I'd caught flu in Malaysia and was feeling really rough. I went to the airport in KL as early as I could and bought everything in the pharmacy I could find to make me sleep. I got on the plane as early as possible and settled myself into my comfy business class seat. The first passenger on and I can generally sleep anywhere at any time – half man, half mattress. I was buckled up and asleep before the second passenger got on.

I came round briefly and saw that business class was full. I woke up again later, realized the flight was still on the ground, that business class was now half empty and wondered why the cabin crew were in bits - crying and comforting each other. But I was too ill, and too sleepy, to wonder for long.

I woke up properly coming into land at Schipol the next morning. My phone erupted with texts from people who had heard on the news, "Malaysian Airlines, Kuala Lumpur, Amsterdam", but not necessarily in that order.

Minutes before takeoff, already on the taxiway, the MH16 crew had heard that MH17 had been lost. They returned to the terminal. Not knowing the cause, they gave all the passengers the opportunity to get off. I had slept through that bit. They then rerouted far to the south of Ukraine. I slept through that bit too. The aircrew at this point knew all their colleagues had been killed.

I'd taken MH16 that night. Seven days before I'd taken MH17. I'd say that's life number 6.

Earlier that year I'd been in Cairo. I'd flown KLM from Amsterdam. A few minutes after takeoff, there had been a flash of white light outside the window. A bit of bouncing around and a few shrieks. We'd been hit by lightning.

A few minutes later the Dutch pilot made an announcement. In his most commanding, most intellectual and most patronizing voice he said:

"As some of you may have concluded, we were hit by lightning". He clearly had a PhD in stating the obvious. "As you will know, an aeroplane is designed to act as a Faraday cage". He knew that no one would know that. But we were still flying, and dinner was being served, so no big deal.

He sounded like an arse.

"All our systems are working perfectly, so we can say that everything functioned as it is designed to do". There was a bit more blah, blah. He intended to sound reassuring and knowledgeable. Instead he sounded like an arse.

Twenty minutes later, another announcement,

"Some of our systems appear to be malfunctioning". "Possibly as a result of the lightning strike". No shit. What happened to Faraday and his cage? "We will be making a precautionary landing in Paris". He was an arse. We landed, waited in Paris for the plane to be checked, and twelve hours later got on another one.

He was an arse.

I'd been lucky enough to go diving in Principe. A bunch of us had hired a small business jet, to take us and our dive gear from Gabon to Sao Tome – the next island over. The pilot warned us that the runway in Sao Tome was short. Planes have a stall warner – it's a klaxon that sounds when the plane is flying too slow, the flight controls are about to become useless, shortly followed by the plane falling out of the sky.

To land on a short runway, you have to be touching down right at the start of the runway and be going as slowly as possible. We were still over the sea, at about 50 feet, when the stall warner went off, and the plane just fell onto the beginning of the runway. What that crew had to do to land in Sao Tome I guess.

I've said before that there was nothing much to do in Gabon. Some years before I arrived, three expatriates had imported a microlight aircraft. Microlights have a triangular fabric wing, two seats – one behind the other. The front seat is for the passenger, who sits between the legs of the rear passenger. The rear passenger is the pilot. There is no cabin or cockpit as such. The pilot controls the flight by pushing forward and backward on an aluminium bar, that tilts the wing. The throttle is a handle on the bar. The engine, mounted behind the pilot, pushes the microlight forward. In technical terms, they're a bit on the flimsy side.

The three expats had taught themselves to fly. Over the years, they had left one by one, until only one was still there. He was my boss. He was also due to leave shortly.

Three of us - all newly arrived expats - agreed to buy the flimsylight. We thought it would keep us busy, but we'd never been in one before. A small issue. We found someone in Libreville who claimed to be an instructor. We could fly him down to us for weekends and he could teach us to fly. Brilliant.

In the meantime, we took turns going out flying with my boss. He was teaching us what he could. It was my turn to go out flying after work that day. At lunchtime, he came in and said his son was travelling back to school in the UK the next day. Would I mind if we postponed our flight until the following day. He wanted to take his son flying before he left. Of course, no worries.

They went flying. They didn't come back.

In the coming days, we all stopped work to walk line abreast through the rainforest looking for them. Teams went out to all the beaches in case they had landed there. Teams went out to all the clearings in the rainforest. The foreign legion sent a hundred legionnaires to help with the search. The company plane diverted to search. A helicopter was chartered to fly search patterns at low level.

They weren't found. Not for a week. My boss enjoyed flying low over "Hippo Lake". The view of the hippos from 25 feet was amazing. This day he hadn't cleared the trees at the edge of Hippo Lake.

My boss's wife and other children were distraught of course. The effect on the small expat community was truly profound.

I think of that often, and consider it life #6.

I had a business trip to a remote location in Bangladesh. Singapore Airlines to Dhaka. Overnight in Dhaka. Domestic flight – I won't name the airline – to Chittagong. I turned up for the domestic flight. It was a small twin propellor aircraft. As I walked out to the steps a mechanic was fitting bits back on the left engine. While we were on the plane, he was frantically stemming an oil leak. I'm not a nervous flyer.

People started to stow hand luggage on the overhead shelf. Seems there was rat up there. The steward chased the rat up and down the plane. It was a fast rat. It took my mind off the oil leak. Surprisingly, we landed in Chittagong without drama. But the first job was to make a phone call - I wasn't taking that plane back to Dhaka. My first, and only refusal.

... chased the rat up and down the plane

I doubt the rat survived long with that gaff – and I was surprised I did. Perhaps life #7?

I stayed at the Hotel Agricole in Chittagong. There was a power cut, so the hotel was in darkness as I arrived. Not even emergency lights. Checked in by torch. Had to pay a deposit for the mini bar – a bit odd, but ok. I was on the first floor. I found my room using the one-inch blue screen from an early mobile phone.

The room was in darkness. It was dark outside. I explored the walls of my room using the fireman's right-hand search method. It really was that dark. You run your right hand along every wall, taking every turn there is, the theory being that eventually you will get back to where you started. You tap the floor in front of you with a foot to make sure the floor is still there. Took me ten minutes to get round the perimeter of my room. My eyes had adjusted a bit, so I took a diagonal across the room towards the mysterious fridge-come-minibar. I'd abandoned the right hand on the wall, and the foot tapping in front of me. That was an error.

Halfway across the diagonal, in a rush to see what my deposit had got me, there was a rug. I stepped on the rug and my foot went through the wooden floor. And the ceiling above reception. I hadn't created the hole – I'd just found it. Cunningly hidden by the well-placed rug. Well you would, wouldn't you.

There was nothing in the fridge except air. A deposit well spent.

Work completed, and due to fly back from Chittagong to Dhaka. Picked up by private jet. It rounded off the Bangladesh adventure perfectly with no further threat to life.

By now, I'd decided I needed to learn to fly. I found the world's friendliest flight school, with the world's most competent instructor, on a farm close to where I lived. The instructor had been a farmer, but his flying hobby, had become a habit, and had taken over. Accomplished glider pilot. Accomplished balloon pilot. He'd learnt to fly in the days when, "a good day's flying … was when the engine kept going all day".

... the engine kept going all day.

Dave was broad Yorkshire. A wicked sense of humour, behind a dead pan expression. He had a side kick, Maurice. Equally broad Yorkshire, himself a very accomplished pilot.

Maurice did the building and maintenance work around the place. And cut the grass on the runways. Dave did all the flying, Maurice did all the work.

I'd got as far as going solo before. At Teesside airport. One day the instructor just said, "go solo now – one circuit". And he got out. One circuit is a takeoff into wind, a left turn, another left turn, a flight parallel to the runway, a left turn, another left turn, then you are on approach to the runway again.

You are so busy taxiing out, getting permission from the tower to line up on the runway, take off roll, climb out – that you don't have time to think. You turn left and then left again. At that point you radio the tower again giving intention to land. After that, you have a few minutes to take in the enormity of the situation. You are on your todd and there's only you that can land the plane, and you, in one piece. It focuses the mind.

The tower had been briefed that I was doing my first solo. Numpty in the circuit, they look after you, don't hassle you and keep everything else out of your way. I landed. First solo complete. Intrepid flying ace.

A week or two later, I did my second solo circuit. "you can solo again now – about 40 minutes to dusk – plenty of time for one quick circuit". The tower doesn't know that you are on your second ever solo circuit and therefore still a numpty in a plane. As far as they are concerned you are a fully competent and highly experienced pilot with thousands of hours in the logbook. You are busy taxiing out, lining up, talking to the tower, take off roll, climb out, left turn, left turn, radio for permission to land. And then you remember that it's all up to you again. A bit of cold sweat broke out. Then the tower called me that, "There's a military plane ten miles out with a technical problem, orbit until further notice". So, to give the sick military plane space, I had to do tight, banked circles, until told otherwise.

I did as told. All the time the wind, and my own inaccuracy, was blowing me away from the runway. I'd never been this far from the airfield on my own before. I saw the military plane land ok and then stop on the runway. And it stayed there. I radioed the tower for permission to land. I was told to fly parallel to the runway away from the airfield, for a "long final". I did.

The lights were on for the runway now – just as well as I couldn't see it without. I put lights on for the plane – I'd never done that before. Sometimes I vaguely thought I should know what all the buttons and knobs did. It was dark enough that I couldn't see the military plane anymore. I was so far away that I couldn't see the runway over my shoulder, even with the lights. I did a bit of pleading with the tower. I don't remember if I used my alternative declaration of emergency. "I'm shitting myself". I think it helped that my instructor was hassling the tower too – worried about his plane I expect. I got permission to land. If only I could find the airport. All I could see were the lights of the nearby city. Eventually the runway lights came into view, but by now, my second ever solo landing had become my first night landing.

It was no problem. But if that wasn't life #8, I don't know what is.

I found Dave. And Maurice. I bought a share in a plane. And I let Dave pass on his wisdom. We did all the flight skills. I passed the theory tests. I passed the flight test. I passed the medical. Suddenly, I was a pilot with a plane. And the airfields of Yorkshire were my oyster.

THE TROLLEY WHEEL

In Oman, I worked a week in the desert. Then had a week off with my family at home in the capital city. Every week I took a two-hour company charter flight to work. Every week I took the return flight home. The capital of Oman had a modern international airport. The oilfield in the desert had a sand airstrip. We used 50-seater, twin propellor, overhead wing, aircraft. Robust and reliable – most of the time.

It was about an 800km flight from the oilfield to the capital. The first 600km over flat gravel plain, and we flew at 4 or 5 thousand feet. The last 200km was a climb over the 10,000-foot mountains, and then the descent into the airport. I had taken that flight every week for five years, so I was attuned to every sound, every change in level, every change in engine note.

We took off from the oilfield desert strip. I slept for 90 minutes. Half man - half mattress. I woke briefly as we started the climb to clear the mountains. I woke again as the engine note dropped for us to descend on the other side. I woke again as I heard the hydraulic whirr of the wheels coming down. A few seconds later, I heard the hydraulic whirr of the wheels going back up again. That wasn't normal - I was completely awake now. Mattress discarded.

A minute later, the hydraulic whirr as the wheels came down yet again. Looking out of the windows, I could see two wheels. A minute later the whirr as wheels went up again. A change of course as we broke off from the approach to the runway. Clearly something wrong.

We flew around a bit more. More whirring. And an announcement. "We didn't get a green light for the nose

115

wheel. We've tried putting it down and up a few times. We've flown past the control tower. They've confirmed we don't have a nosewheel."

I was already uncomfortable.

"We've spoken to the engineers, and they've suggested we try a monoeuvre that you may find uncomfortable". I was already uncomfortable. Half the passengers were not English speakers – they knew something was wrong – they didn't know what – they were uncomfortable.

We flew in very tight banked circles. Enough to push your guts down in your seat. At the same time the whirring was going on – wheels down. The thought in my mind, "It'll be ok this time". More whirring as wheels went back up. It obviously wasn't alright this time. We did this a few times. And then we flew out over the sea. We could see the pilots leafing through manuals. For anyone who thinks there is a little windy handle that you turn, and the wheels go down. There isn't.

"We are going to try another manoeuvre." This one involved climbing, then diving steeply. Then pulling up sharply. Arse pushed into seat. Guts pushed into arse. Head weighing a couple of tonnes. At the same time, a bunch of hydraulic whirring. We did this a few times. It was obviously not working. Off out over the sea again for a bit of a think.

"We are going to make an emergency landing. But first we need to dump fuel. The cabin crew will get you to practice the brace position. We will move people around in the cabin to balance the plane. We will come into land as slowly as possible. As we touch down, we will cut all electrical supplies. We will cut the engines. We will hold the nose up as long as possible.

You will see the fire trucks on the runway. Don't evacuate the plane if you can see flames. Don't evacuate until you are told to". Simples. But not your average Friday.

I would rather have been anywhere else. But that wasn't an option.

It's fair to say that there was some tension. We did a bit of practice bracing and shifted people around. We were streaming fuel. There couldn't have been much left – a two-hour flight was already three and a half. Eventually, "We are making an approach to land, take the brace position". And we did. Until, "There's a commercial aircraft 20 miles out and they'd like to land that before us". As if to say, "We'll make such a mess of their runway, they want to get the airliner down first while they can". So, we broke away from the approach and went round again. Another little turn on the tension knob.

This time we approached to land. We took the brace position. We were noticeably slow. The main wheels touched down. All the lighting went off – pitch black. The engines cut – complete silence. The pilot held the nose up. At a certain point it dropped suddenly. The nose scraped along the runway – the noise was intense – the light from sparks outside the windows was blinding. Like someone welding outside my window.

We screeched to a halt. The plane was full of smoke. Evacuation order given. I went through the underwing exit. The rear emergency door, with the nose on the tarmac, was 20 feet in the air. There was no fire. The fire trucks were there. Emergency service helicopters flew overhead. We stood on the sand at the side of the runway and congratulated each other on being alive.

Any moment, someone would come and tell us what to do. The fire crew sprayed some foam around. A special cradle arrived, and they started winching the nose of the plane up, to put it on the cradle, so they could tow it away. We were about a kilometer away from the terminal building – we could see the lights in the distance. We gave up waiting and walked to the terminal building. The door I usually went in was locked. So, we knocked. Then knocked loudly. A scene from Monty Python. Eventually it opened and we were allowed in.

We weren't allowed to leave the terminal though. I assumed that we'd be interviewed. I thought we'd probably be given a medical. And then we'd be taken home. Or placed under psychological evaluation. No .... we couldn't leave because we had luggage to reclaim. I got my bag. I walked out of the terminal. I got in my car. I drove myself the 20 kilometers home.

When I was late home, my wife had phoned the airport. The emergency number that we all gave our families. No one had answered for a few calls. When someone did answer there was a lot of nervous muttering, no information and the instruction to phone back later. Possibly not as reassuring as it could have been.

I was used to getting two or three work calls a day in my week off. I thought someone might call to see how I was doing after the excitement. That week .... not one phone call. A week later I went to the airport and got on a different plane. The same flight back to work. I knew an expat who was badly affected and wouldn't fly. Several of the local staff decided they weren't flying again.

Back at work and the landing incident was the subject of much talk. At a certain point, I mentioned that I'd been on that flight. No one knew. There had been no passenger list, so no one was ever going to phone anyone to see if they were ok. I was though – ok that is - not bothered in any way that I could notice. I said to my boss over lunch," when does my counselling start". He put his arm round my shoulder, said," there, there – counselling finished". And that was that.

... there, there ... counselling finished.

It wasn't quite. The boys in the bar thought the event needed marking. Later that week, they did a presentation. Someone had made a nice piece of polished wood. Somewhere they'd found a shopping trolley wheel. Somehow, they'd done a brass plaque, "Oman Air 15, 17 May 1995". The free beer and the piss taking were better than any counselling. I've still got that plaque.

Life # 9. I didn't know whether to stop counting.

Years later, flying my own plane, Dave the instructor was in the passenger seat. Every year I had to do a flight test to revalidate my license. We'd finished the test and were flying back to the airfield. Coming into land, I was flying at 800 feet – for anyone that doesn't know – that's not very high – you can recognize people on the ground. Two Harrier jump jets flew past underneath us at mach-whatever-they-do. I didn't recognise the pilots – they didn't look in my direction, at all - but I could have polished their helmets without stretching.

Dave and me sat on two rocking chairs on the verandah of the shed that we called the flying club. We were good friends and we sat in companionable silence enjoying bright sunshine, the green of the Yorkshire countryside and celebrating the fact we were still alive. A theme.

Dave was enjoying his sit down and a cuppa. Maurice was working. He had been using the tractor and trailer to shift bags of cement from one side of the airfield to the other. Those bags that weigh 25 kilos each – they're heavy. Maurice stopped the tractor with the second load of bags and started carrying them, one by one, over to the path he was laying.

Dave was talking to himself under his breath, but loud enough so I could hear. *Mind ... he is 82* "Come on Maurice, you useless bugger, pep it up … can't believe how long it's taking him to shift those bags." A few seconds silence and then Dave turned to me, "mind … he is 82".

I've sold my plane now and I've stopped flying. Nine lives weren't enough. And there are more adventurous things I want to do.

CHAPTER ELEVEN

Beating A Bastard, Garbage and Fences

I'M MOTIVATED BY challenge. The more diverse the better. And variety. I'd been on Siberia channel 7 TV many times. I got recognized on the train as that "foreigner from the oilfield". So, when the latest invitation appeared to be interviewed, I made it a mission to think of something different to do, that didn't involve me.

We did some genuinely great sustainable development work with the nearby village. I was in the village often, I was the face of the company there, and I felt a personal responsibility to the villagers. They had made me so welcome, I wanted to do good work with them, and for them. There was one idea I took genuine joy from.

The young people in the village left school at 17. Like many rural areas around the world, if they were smart enough, they left for University. On graduation, with all the employment prospects in the cities, they didn't come back. The population was ageing. We decided to sponsor ten school leavers, through a well-respected oil and gas University. We selected the school leavers carefully, with the help of both schools. We gave the students vacation time work experience. A few years later, when the first students became graduates, we started offering jobs to the best ones.

It wasn't my idea — I wished it was.

It meant we helped give young villagers qualifications. The qualifications meant they had a career for life. It meant we could reduce the number of people we employed from outside of the region. It meant that whoever we employed would stay in the village and they would have a good disposable income. It wasn't my idea – I wished it was. But I sponsored the whole thing and made sure it happened. I was extremely proud of the programme, the process and the graduates. So was my friend Vitali, the mayor.

The channel 7 crew arrived. We set them up to film at a wellhead. I had invited one of our best village graduates to come. We met the mayor at the wellhead. I had asked the graduate to explain the finer workings of the wellhead to his mayor, and answer any questions he might have had, in front of the channel 7 cameras.

I don't know who was the proudest person that day. The graduate demonstrating the knowledge, skills and career that he had achieved. Or Vitali - there was literally a tear in his eye as he listened to one of his young villagers – he'd known him since he was a toddler. Or me – I played no part in the whole interview, which was exactly what I wanted.

We did some less successful sustainable development stuff too. I had four hospitals in the field, run by a medical team leader, and a plethora of doctors and nurses. One year, for the week of International AIDS day, someone clever thought we should run an AIDS awareness campaign in the field and in the village. Part of this included putting out bulk packs of condoms all over the place. Packs of 250. I didn't know we were doing it, so when the medical team leader came to me and said several thousand condoms had been taken, I was all ready to investigate theft. When he explained, I could only think there was more of a social life in the field than I'd have guessed.

But no, both assumptions were wrong – over the coming days, condoms, blown up like balloons, appeared stuck to every noticeboard, window, door handle, vehicle aerial, fence post and handrail. It wasn't only one office that was filled by inflated condoms whilst the occupant went for lunch. It was a bit of a struggle to explain what was going on to visitors that week.

The troops were telling us that there was no lack of AIDS awareness in rural Russia and to think otherwise was just a little bit arrogant. And they had a point. I quite liked the originality of the protest, so just laughed. It brightened up a tough shift. Oh – and the other reason may have been that the condoms someone had bought had the consistency of car tyres. Unusable for even the toughest of Siberians. That was another weird conversation.

... condoms .... The consistency of car tyres.

Someone – possibly the same person that selected the condoms - decided we needed company branded volleyballs as a giveaway. Nice idea – everyone liked getting this type of stuff. A thousand would have been reasonable. But at least one "0" and maybe two, got added to the order. The supplier kept quiet – he was a happy chappy. And for whatever reason, they were delivered already blown up. This vast quantity, and volume, was delivered to a warehouse in Moscow.

I think pencils must have snapped at the cost of warehousing thousands and thousands of ready blown up volleyballs, while someone figured out what to do with them. So I was asked if we could put them somewhere in the field. Always ready to make the most of a really good cock-up, I said yes. Shortly afterwards ten full size shipping containers of volleyballs arrived. And I spent the next 5 years giving them to anyone that would take ten. A couple of hundred miles from the field, I'd be on the train, looking out of the window, and every garden I passed, would have a branded volleyball in it. I took dozens back to Europe with me – I found one recently on the roof of my house, twenty years after I must have brought it home. I kept a couple in the corridor outside my office. If I needed to think, I'd dribble it up and down the corridor, noisily, in my slippers, annoying everyone.

In Gabon, I got out of my Louis XIV bed one morning. It hadn't been quite as Louis XIV since the snake and shotgun event. In the office, we all wore overalls – as well as the guys actually working with the tools. So, first thing I did was put on my overalls. No one was that fussy about appearances, so it took about 90 seconds to get ready for the day. I stepped outside, straight into my LandRover. I drove round the corner, and there was the fire chief. Surprisingly, he wasn't eating, sleeping or polishing his fire truck.

He was standing outside of his room, in his underpants, beating his overalls with a broom handle. This was a little unusual even for Gabon. I thought about stopping to see if he was ok. But I knew that whatever the problem was, it would come into my office at sometime during the day. So, I just drove past and gave him a little wave. Uncharacteristically, he was too busy with the broomstick to notice.

In later years I became a regular visitor to Malaysia, usually Borneo Island. This time, I flew from Kuala Lumpur to Miri in Sarawak. The plane landed in Kuching en route. Everyone had to get off and wandered around the terminal for an hour. Then got back on the same plane to finally arrive in Miri. Malaysia is full of hospitable, can-do people – I loved going there. Kuching departure is not overrun by amenities. But it does have toilets. I went to the toilet, and as I was walking in, two men walked out. One of them was wearing military fatigues. The other one was wearing blue trousers and a white t shirt. They were handcuffed together. One clearly a guard and one clearly a prisoner. The pair in transit somewhere. My jet lagged brain ticked over. I wondered how that had worked out … were they in a cubicle? or if they were at a urinal, who did what, for who, and how? So many questions unanswered.

Before getting back on the plane, I went to the toilet again. There really was nothing else to do. As I walked out, another guard, handcuffed to a prisoner, walked in. The guard's left hand was handcuffed to the prisoners right. As I walked on, I registered what was different about this pair. The prisoner only had one arm – his left arm amputated just below the shoulder. As I walked on a bit further, I started to picture who was going to do what and for who in that pairing. I went through all the combinations I could think of – they were all challenging. Outstanding co-operation between guard and prisoner.

A few steps further on, and I convinced myself I needed

my curiosity satisfying. I turned to go back to the toilet. Then I thought how wrong this would be in so many ways. I had a word with myself, gave my head a shake and left guard and prisoner to figure it out without my help. But I often wonder.

In Russia, there is a technical law that says you must have a loudspeaker in every occupied area. In the event of a fire alarm, a recorded message played. The recorded message told you what to do. I felt this a bit surplus to requirements, since there was a deafening, and specific, fire claxon. Nevertheless, a rule is a rule

My arse is on fire — I'm leaving — so should you.

In new offices, someone has to record the message. Since we had many Russian speakers, but also a few non-Russian speakers, we needed a message in English and in Russian. My PA recorded the Russian message, "There's a fire, get out", or something like that. And the honour of recording the English version fell to me. "My arse is on fire – I'm leaving – so should you". It seemed appropriate, it was somehow much more personal, and it gave me a laugh every time we had a false alarm. And not against the rules.

Back in Gabon. After I'd seen the fire chief whacking his overalls with a broomstick, I went to the office. Later that day, someone mentioned the fire chief had had a run in with a snake. We religiously reported all incidents, and I was encouraging people to do exactly that. Not everyone knew how to do it, which sometimes put them off. I thought I'd help the fire chief – he could eat, sleep and supervise polishing, but I was sure he couldn't use the reporting system. I got someone to go through the input forms with him, and he agreed to break into his eating, sleeping and polishing routine, to supply the details. He was a French only speaker, and the system allowed only English, so I was anticipating some fun. Later that day I went through his report with him.

Date of incident:	17th May
Time of incident:	06:15
Place of incident:	Camp, outside room C22
Description of incident:	I collected my overalls from the laundry on the evening of 16th of May. I put the overalls on the chair next to my bed. I went to sleep. At 06:00 I woke up and put my overalls on. They felt strange, so I put my hands in the front pockets. I felt a snake there.
Immediate action:	I ripped my overalls off. I threw them outside. I beat the bastard to death.

All the information was there. Nothing wrong with the detail. English correct. I didn't know if the snake knew its parents, but I judged it followed all the rules. I thought about editing it, in anticipation of management review. Nah.

I beat the bastard to death.

Broomsticks would have been useless in Siberia. We were getting lots of bear visits into the camps. They were looking for anything edible. And were skilled at getting into any sort of garbage container – no matter how secure an area we put them in, no matter what clever bear proof catches we fitted. We had alert systems for every time a bear entered a camp. But with camps the size of villages and no perimeter fences, there were lots of opportunities for a resourceful bear or three.

We had sophisticated systems for keeping wild animals out of the refuse area. First it was birds that were forever foraging in there. So, we got acoustic bird scarers. A continuously recorded sound of a bird in distress. Not sure what it did for the birds, but for the humans it was white noise torture. In fairness, it did keep the birds away. However, it did attract the dogs and wolves – they came to see what was up with the birds. So, we got acoustic dog scarers – fortunately, I couldn't hear those. I did wonder if we'd switched them on. But in fairness, it did keep the dogs away. There were two opposite theories from the bear experts. Theory number one – always have a dog around, because they will alert you to approaching bears. Theory number two – don't have a dog, because it's like bear bait – walking dinner. For sure, the acoustic dog scarer, attracted the bears. We never got as far as acoustic bear scarers and whatever they'd attract.

We had one specific remote camp that was a problem. That camp was having bear visitors just about every night. So, we bit the bullet and decided to build a bear proof perimeter fence. Bears are territorial – once they've taken up residence, they are hard to shift. And a whole family of bears had taken up residence around, and more worryingly, in, that camp.

... three bears — yes really ...

We hired a local contractor to build the fence. We had a local hunter watch over the crew as they were building the fence, just in

128

case. The edge of the forest was twenty metres from the line of the fence. The three bears – yes really, three – sat just inside the forest, watching the fence being built with interest.

At a certain point I got an emergency call. Bear attack in the middle of the day at the camp where we were building the fence. We got into emergency response mode. Afterwards we investigated what had happened.

One of the crew who were building the bear exclusion fence had been attacked by one of the bears. He survived, but he had been badly mauled. Having the hunter there had saved his life – he'd fired in the general direction of the bear, and the bear had naffed off. At a certain point, the fence builder had left the fence line. He needed to go to the toilet. So, he went into the forest. One of the watching bears had attacked him.

Once I knew the guy was safe, I had two thoughts. Thought number one: there were two sides to the bear fence - why would anyone building a bear fence decide to go on the bear side of the fence. Thought number two: the phrase, "Does a bear shit in the woods", could never be the same for me.

We had bears that preferred to shit in a camp. And a man that preferred to shit in the woods.

After five years in Siberia, I'd learned a lot about how things work, or don't, in low temperatures. At that time, we had mercury temperature gauges all over the field – we didn't have digital gauges. Mercury gauges only read the temperature to minus fifty degrees centigrade. We had one seven-day period when nothing registered on a gauge anywhere in the field. We didn't know how cold it got; we just knew it was colder than minus fifty for seven complete days. Even the Russians looked at each other and shrugged – even they didn't know what would happen.

I was asked by an international trade body to come and tell them what it meant to operate an oilfield in low temperatures. This was picked up by the UK Department of Trade and Industry. They had me present to UK contractors who were bidding for work in arctic environments. I went on to write, "Operating an Oilfield at Minus Fifty Degrees C". As books go, it's heavy going – this one is better.

As books go .... This one is better

By the time it was published and companies were talking to me about it, I'd been reassigned to Egypt. Some challenge to establish credibility in the field of arctic expertise, when you're talking from the Egyptian Western desert.

A LONG NIGHT AT THE MOVIES

Before I left Siberia, I was invited to Vitaly's house, the mayor, for dinner. It was genuinely a treat and a privilege for me. I'd come to terms with his banya. As I drove up to Vitaly's house, I was looking forward to a relaxed dinner with an old friend and his family.

Vitaly's family were as welcoming as always. We were chatting before dinner, and I remarked to Vitaly that I hadn't heard from him for a few weeks. He'd been on vacation. That explained it. He'd been to Mineralnya Vodi – a city several hundred kilometers from Salym. Mineralnya Vodi translates as "Mineral Waters". Although I had never been, I knew it had been a favoured spa resort, with sanatoriums where, in time past, the communist party faithful, had been rewarded with state funded summer vacations. That had all been in a past era of course. I was interested in Mineralnya Vodi and even more interested why Vitaly had chosen to go there. So, I asked him all about it.

He said that the best way he could explain, would be to show me. He went to another room. He came back with a white carrier bag. He took out a camcorder. It was a state-of-the-art camcorder then but would look old fashioned now – a fold out two-inch screen, with mini video tape cassettes. It had been Vitaly's new toy just before going on vacation. He was proud of it.

I asked how he had travelled. He'd gone by coach. How long had it taken? Just over two days. Each way. That would have been absolute torture for me, but Vitaly was clearly so enthusiastic about it.

Vitaly found a tape and he showed me on the mini screen. It was the coach trip. He had used the coach trip to experiment with all the features of his new camcorder. White light, split screen, slow motion. But mostly videoing the back of the head of the man in the seat in front. For two days. We watched most of it. We must have fast forwarded, but it didn't feel like it.

Then we watched another tape. Finally, we had arrived in Mineralnya Vodi. This tape was arriving at the sanatorium. Vitaly had been experimenting with point of view videoing. This was before anyone had heard the term, point of view. So, with the camcorder held up to his eye, I watched him collect his bag from the coach, walk into reception, check in, collect his key and walk along several corridors to his room.

Bizarrely, in Russia, hotel room doors open out into the corridor. And they have heavy springs to shut them behind you.

I watched Vitaly struggle to open the door – camcorder held up to his eye, turning the key, opening the door against the spring, picking up his bag, walking in. At this point he had stopped to video the entrance to his room. But he'd stopped a few inches too early. The door shut violently and whacked him on the back of the head, still with camcorder welded to his eye. So, there were a few moments of juddering, a bit of staggering about, carpet came into closeup view and some classic Russian swearing.

He'd stopped a few inches too early.

Unusually for a Russian, Vitaly could laugh at himself. He did. Me too.

There were a lot of cassettes in that carrier bag. We watched another one. This one was Vitaly doing point of view videoing around his room. We saw the bathroom, the shower, the toilet, the bidet and a toothbrush. We saw a test flush of the toilet, but mercifully, none of the amenities were being used in anger during the filming. But I did wonder what was coming next.

The highlight was the room telephone. It was one of those with a numbered dial, where you put your fingertip in the dial and turned it as far as a metal stop. For good measure, Vitaly rang the 10 digits of his home number in Salym, to talk to his family. Not easy with a camcorder to your eye and it took a few attempts to get the number right. He captured the whole dialing experience, a couple of wrong numbers and the long conversation with his family – well his half of the conversation anyway. It was riveting. But I was losing the will to live a bit.

Mount Elbrus is the highest mountain in Europe. But only if

you draw the Europe/Asia boundary in a certain way. Vitaly had done a day's outing, from Mineralnya Vodi to Mount Elbrus. By coach. I knew of Mount Elbrus but had never been there or seen photographs. There was a lot of videoing in the coach again. Although the head and hair in front were someone else, which was exciting. I was pleased though when we pulled up in the coach park at the base of Mount Elbrus. The coach park turned out to be at the bottom station of a cable car. The weather was beautiful as Vitaly got into the cable car – he was wearing shorts, t-shirt, a big smile and a baseball cap. He'd moved on to doing still selfies. The camcorder was still attached to his right eye. So, I had the opportunity to study the inside of the cable car in detail – every rivet.

Turned out that this cable car went only part way up the mountain, to an intermediate station. We all got off the cable car and walked the hundred metres to the bottom of a modern four-man chairlift. I felt I was there. It was modern, but slow, so we went through two or three seasons on the way up to the top. It was obviously quite chilly, and very misty, as, half an hour later, I got off the chairlift with Vitaly.

Turned out that this chairlift went only part way to the summit as well. It's not the highest mountain in Europe for nothing. There was quite a long discussion amongst Vitaly's chums, about a further chairlift that went further up the mountain. They knew it was there but couldn't see it because of the mist. Neither could I. Watching a video of mist is not the most rewarding thing I've done.

Most of the group decided they weren't going further up. But Vitaly, a few diehards and his camcorder bravely set off searching in the mist for the third chairlift. They found it. There was

Vitaly and his shorts were not deterred.

more than a hint of snow on the ground. A big warning sign filled the screen. The warning sign told of changeable weather, the need to be properly equipped and the danger of hypothermia. However, Vitaly and his shorts were not deterred.

I got on the chairlift with Vitaly and his camcorder. It was an ancient one-man chairlift. It was moving slower than the glaciers that came into the camcorders view after twenty minutes or so. This would be a couple of cassettes worth. I knew Vitaly was getting cold because his right hand was starting to shiver, the camcorder was shaking all over the place and the mist was out of focus. Apart from that it was great video.

The chairlift stopped for a few moments. As they do sometimes. Vitaly swung up and down as the cable settled. The camcorder shook more and more violently as Vitaly shivered more and more. It was snowing. A couple of cassettes later he got off at the top. His one or two chums who were in the chairs in front of him, had icicles on their hair and in their beards.

It was midnight by this time. We'd had a massive amount of fun, in a masochistic kind of way. But I really did need to be up early tomorrow. We'd got a long way through Vitaly's carrier bag, but not to the bottom. Vitaly's good humour and enthusiasm for everything was infectious. But when he picked up a cassette and said that he'd got much better with the camcorder during the two-day return coach trip from Mineralnya Vodi to Salym, my face must have collapsed.

Let's save that for another time, he said.

CHAPTER TWELVE

Trumpets, Tehran and Terrified

YOU KNOW HOW you get invitations for something you look forward to, invitations that aren't really invitations, and invitations where you'd rather go to the dentist for a bit of root canal?

One of the many ways that you could fall foul of Gina the local immigration police chief, in Siberia, was by having the wrong medical certificate. You needed a medical certificate to go with your annual work permit. The medical certificate had nothing to do with checking your health. It had everything to do with making money for the Russian state. It had a little bit to do with stopping foreigners bringing disease into the country.

The first couple of medicals were at a government clinic in Moscow. I was tested for every communicable disease there is. And some imaginary ones. It was the most intimate and invasive examination possible. It took all day. It made prison strip searches look casual. It was the same Russian doctor every time, sticking his fingers in the same orifices – all of them. Not all of his fingers – all of my orifices. I dreaded it. I came to think of him as Doctor Digit. But I guess my once a year penance was nothing compared to just how shit his average week must have been.

I came to think of him as Dr. Digit

I got invited to judge the Miss Salym competition. I told the whole team at work of course – there was a lot of jealousy and a lot of piss taking – which was the idea. Nothing creates a better team feeling, than taking the piss out of the boss. I let them each think I might send them instead of me. Just toying with them. My little joke. But come the day, I headed off into Salym myself. Well you would.

My Russian was good, but not by any means perfect. So, I'd missed a couple of nuances in the invitation. I hadn't realised that all the contestants would be between 7 and 11. Years of age. It was an afternoon of trumpet playing, tap dancing, the odd violin, dodgy poetry recital in Russian, and an act with a cat that I never did understand. I told my team I'd had a great time, and no more. I sent someone else the next year. Well you would.

To get to Tehran, I needed endless letters of invitation. And endless patience. And persistence. Which is ironic because I didn't really want to go. I ended up with a passport stuck in the Iranian embassy in Amsterdam on a Friday afternoon, due to travel to Tehran on Monday, and wanting to go home to Yorkshire for the weekend.

I was going to Tehran with a colleague – I'll call him Ed. Ed was Dutch, a technical genius, a truly nice guy and an old friend. But he could be a walking disaster. In all the years I'd known him, he had never had a complete shave – he always missed a bit and the bit he'd missed was always an inch long. But it was a different bit every day. He'd have an inch-long tuft in one place today, and then an inch-long tuft somewhere else, the next. I never did figure out how he did that.

THE WORLD (NOT MUCH OF IT)

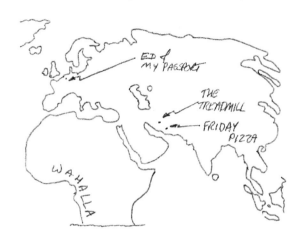

RUSSIA (YOU KNEW THAT)

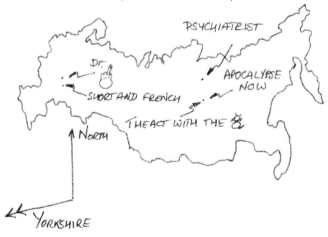

We had a clear desk policy. Except for Ed's office. It was stacked waist high everywhere with documents, books and files. When he went on a trip, someone would swill it out and find all sorts of lost treasures. A rumour of rats on one occasion.

I phoned him one night because he was late to meet for dinner. He answered his mobile. And all I heard was the sound of Ed falling off his bike. The bleeps of an incomplete call. And a wounded and disheveled Ed arrived five minutes later. With a bent bike. Should have been wearing a helmet, but he was Dutch. 'Nuff said.

He once went home to Holland for the weekend from Moscow. Washing his hands before leaving his flat, he pulled the handle off the cold tap. With no way to shut off the water, no spare time to fix it and a slightly warped logic, he just left it running for the long weekend. It was always a worry when I knew I was travelling anywhere near Ed.

And the only answer to my passport problem, was for Ed to collect my passport, along with his own, from the Iranian embassy, and meet me in an Amsterdam airport bar. On Monday morning. An hour before the Tehran flight. What could possibly go wrong. Nothing did – he had my passport, he was there, he was on time, he'd had most of a shave and I had a visa. But that was the end of the good news.

So, I slept with Ed. In the hotel gym.

We landed in Tehran late that evening. It took hours to get through formalities. It was twenty minutes by taxi into central Tehran. It was late when we got to the hotel that Ed had booked for both of us. They'd never heard of us. You can't go wandering around Tehran, late at night, as a foreigner, dragging a suitcase, looking for a bed. And by phone, the few hotels that were answering, had no space. So, I slept with Ed. In the hotel gym.

He was curled up under a weights bench, happily snoring and dribbling. I was on a treadmill. I often am – but not usually to sleep. There was an underground car park. Every time a car came or went, the roll up door underneath my treadmill would open with much juddering and screeching. Then it would judder, and screech closed again. And in between the car headlights would shine in my face. Ed slept like a baby, visibly growing tufts of stubble with every passing headlight. By morning we were barely speaking – Ed because he was still half asleep, me because I was brain dead. And it continued like this for the next two weeks as we travelled around Southern Iran looking at engineering stuff.

In Russia, to practice as engineer, you have to pass professional exams. Foreigners too. You had to do the exams in Russian, with a pen and paper. You did the exams at the Moscow head-quarters of the regulatory body Rostechnadzor. So, in my first few weeks in Russia, with no words of Russian, I went to do my exams. You were allowed an interpreter. I thought about some panic studying of the books. There were a lot. But obviously, it doesn't matter what you say in response to a question. It only matters what the interpreter says. Getting the interpreter right was more important than reading the books. I selected my interpreter carefully – he'd passed the exams many times on behalf of many different people. He would translate a question for me. I didn't even understand the question – it would relate to some obscure element of Russian technical law and not actual engineering. We'd chat for a bit in English about something irrelevant. Then he told me he knew the answer. And then he answered. It worked for me.

The exams are available online now, in English, and multiple choice. Taken all the challenge and excitement out of them.

In Gabon, I invited two contractors to take permanent contracts. They were good young guys. I was keen to keep them. An innovation at the time, was that they needed to take a pre-employment medical. This was the mid-nineties. Freddie Mercury had died a few years before. Little was known about HIV anywhere. Virtually nothing was known about HIV in Africa. Except that it was rife.

The company doctor phoned me. One of my guys had failed his pre-employment medical. He had tested positive for HIV. There was no company policy for anything. There definitely wasn't a company policy for HIV positive workers, in remote locations, in shared living environments, in Africa. There was even less real knowledge. There was however a lot of prejudice based on ignorance. The doctor invited me to make up a quick policy. Buck passing in the extreme. I had no idea what to do.

The guy was due to take the company flight back to work the following week. I phoned him. Had the doctor talked to him about the results of his medical? He had. He had said there was something wrong but hadn't really explained what. I told him he needed to go back to the doctor for more explanation. I phoned the doctor and invited him to do his job. Very specifically, the guy needed to stay at home until we understood what we needed to do to make sure there was a safe environment for everyone. Confidentiality didn't exist – and once his condition was known, I'd have a riot on my hands if he was in the field.

I cancelled his flight back to the field. Yes, I know how that looks now, but at the time it seemed like the right thing to do. On balance.

A few days later, the guy walked into my office in the field. I asked him if he'd spoken to the doctor again. He had. What had the doctor said. The doctor had said that he had a disease. But the guy had found, and taken, some natural treatment from a village doctor. And he was ok now. Mmmmmm. His cousin ran the check in for the company flights, so when he'd turned up at the terminal, and wasn't on the flight list, his cousin had been only too happy to solve the problem. Mmmmmm. I phoned the doctor and gave him a further invitation …

In a following year, much to my relief, I didn't have to go to the Moscow clinic for my medical. I didn't have to see my mate Doctor Digit. I had to go to a nearby Siberian city for my medical. The infighting between the Federal authorities and the Regional authorities, for who got the work permit medical money, had obviously been won by Nefteugansk that year. By nearby, I mean 6 hours' drive away with an overnight stay. I wasn't sure my Russian was up to it; I didn't know the names of any of my orifices in Russian. So, I got Svetlana – a translator who lived in Nefteugansk – to meet me at the clinic. I really didn't know how it was going to work having this kind of medical through a translator. It had all the makings of a whitehall farce. But without, I might find myself proffering the wrong orifice to the wrong doctor at the wrong time. And that would be embarrassing.

I didn't know the names of any of my orifices in Russian

Anticipating a long day, we met early the next morning at the wooden hut clinic. We went to reception and an elderly babushka in a white tunic and funny white hat, said some gibberish. "We need to go and see the psychiatrist". I was expecting – hoping – that this medical would be different to the usual. And so far, it was. Maybe I did need to go and see the psychiatrist – it had been a tough trip – and it had been suggested before. But how did they know?

Turned out to be a translational error. I was in the office of the Narcologist. He asked Svetlana his first question. Did I smoke. No. Had I ever smoked. No. Furious note taking – but I'd only said two words and they were both the same. Maybe he was the psychiatrist after all. He asked Svetlana his second question, Did I take drugs – it wasn't clear if he meant illicit drugs or prescription drugs. Either way – no. Had I ever taken drugs. The same ambiguity. We went for a "no" again. Furious note taking. Then, he took on an air of extreme gravity, pen poised, and I braced myself for some seriously searching questions. Did I drink? I drink very little. To lighten the mood, I gave Svetlana the answer to translate. "For six months of the year I'm at work, and I impose a zero-alcohol policy on everyone. Including myself. For the other six months I try and make up for it". Note taking went into overdrive, and I regretted being a smart arse. He asked Svetlana how much I drank in my time off. I really do drink very little, so I gave Svetlana an answer to match. A climax of note taking.

You need to drink more.

The Narcologist leant forward in his chair, I could see him better – the thick pungent smoke from the pipe he'd been smoking thinned a bit as he came closer. He had that big red, veined nose of a lifelong enthusiastic drinker. He looked over his glasses at me, and said, "You need to drink more".

The Narcologist had run out of questions. And that was the end of the medical. No orifices disturbed. Medical passed. Six hours drive back. The invitation for my last medical in Russia was much more fun.

I also had to pass technical exams in Russia, to manage the emergency response teams in the oilfield. The difference with this was that someone from the Russian Ministry of Emergencies came to the field, did a couple of days of view-graphs, then gave you an oral exam. In English. There were about seven of us needed to go through this process. After the first twenty minutes, it was clear that this was going to be dull. It was also clear that we were light years ahead of the Ministry of Emergencies in how we managed emergencies. Sadly, we just had too much practice. And the guy realised it quickly. Like all business travellers in Russia, he needed my signature to say he'd been in my field, to get his expenses. I quite liked that - oh, the power.

So, we came to a deal. If there was one person out of the seven in the room for him to present to, he was happy. So, we turned up by rota, and went back to work when not your turn to sit and listen. We all had to take the exam though. All except me. He didn't think it was appropriate for the actual big boss – the one that sanctioned his expenses - to have to take an exam. Smart bloke, right answer and a great invitation. I accepted.

We were looking forward to leaving Tehran. After two weeks, Ed and I were speaking to each other again. We checked in early. Passports, separate paper visa stamped, boarding cards checked at passport control. All checked again at customs. We went hours early – not to enjoy the amenities at Tehran airport, because there were none, but because we wanted to go home. The plane was late, so in all, we probably had five hours sitting at the departure gate on the only amenity. At last the flight was called. We started to queue to get on. Ed was checking his pockets and his bag. Somewhere in the last five hours sitting in a chair at the gate, he'd lost his passport, visa and boarding card. Nightmare. Could have been worse though. He could have lost my passport somewhere. You don't argue with Iranian border police. So, I got on the plane and Ed was invited to go for a chat with the border police.

The mayor of Salym would phone me. We were, and are, good friends. He would say that we needed a meeting. I would ask where. If he said we should meet at his office, I knew there was an issue. If he said we should meet at the lake, I knew he was fed up with mayoring for the day and wanted some downtime.

There was a sizeable lake at the back of the village – maybe 2 kilometers from end to end. There was a small sand beach, and we would meet there. At some point in the past, someone had donated a small yacht to the mayor's office. On the list of useful things to give a Siberian mayor, a yacht wouldn't have been a strong choice. I think it was with the idea of providing sailing opportunities to the kids of the village. The flaw in the plan was that no one in the village could sail. Vitaly the mayor couldn't sail. But I could. And I was only too happy to escape the oilfield for a few hours, on a trip disguised as work. So, if Vitaly didn't want to be found for a few hours, he'd suggest we meet at the beach, so I could take him sailing, in his yacht. Just the two of us.

We'd had the odd drama – we ran aground on one occasion – but Vitaly just took his tie off, jumped out and pushed us a bit. One specific day, we were mid lake, gliding along, early afternoon, the birds stopped singing, the night lights on the village communication tower came on, and it got very dark, very quickly. We looked at each other – obviously, the apocalypse. Then we remembered there was a solar eclipse and Western Siberia was on the exact path for maximum occlusion.

Obviously, the apocalypse.

Sailing a yacht, on a lake in Siberia, with my good friend the local mayor, in a total eclipse of the sun. An invitation I will never forget.

In West Africa, I worked weekends. And I worked in that satellite office in the compound with the razor wire. Well sometimes it had razor wire. Unless the rugby had been on. There was always potential for general disruption in that area though.

There's a lovely word in West Africa. Wahalla. Any kind of trouble, stress, worry or anxiety, is "Wahalla". Say that and everyone knows what you mean.

One Saturday morning, I came out of my house early to go to the office. No driver. Not unusual, but he would be getting some wahalla. I was pissed off that I had got up early, but the driver slept in, so I would have to hang around an hour for him to turn up. While I was hanging around, I noticed a bullet lodged in the roof of the car – someone had been firing in the air and the car had caught it on the way down. You don't get that in Yorkshire. The driver turned up – yawning. We got in the car. No fuel. More wahalla. Overnight, someone had nicked the fuel. The driver took a jerry can and went on the hunt for fuel. This was not a good day and it had barely started.

We set off for the office late morning. Traffic was bad, so we took a route that skirted the dodgy bit of the town. We made a left turn and must have upset the police who sat there. They wanted us to stop. They had a great method of stopping us and making sure we stayed stopped. One policeman stood in front of the car with his hands on the bonnet. The other let all the air out of two tyres. We were about a kilometer from the office by now. This had the makings of big wahalla. I told the driver he was on his own sorting this out, and I was walking to the office. Walking along the edge of dodgy.

Walking along the edge of dodgy.

I wouldn't normally dream of walking in this area. And I was carrying a laptop. Wearing a watch. A wallet in my pocket. I was conspicuous. A target on my back. I walked quickly avoiding eye contact. I got close to the office compound. There was a high locked steel double gate for car access. Next to that was a guardhouse, manned twenty-four hours a day. The guardhouse had a locked steel entry door. Only this day the door to the guardhouse was wide open. And as I walked up, I could see that the windows in the outside wall were all smashed. Some major wahalla had occurred.

I peered round the door frame. The wooden counter where the guards checked your passes, the desk and chairs where the guards sat – it had all been reduced to matchsticks. No guards. But they usually ran away at the first sign of wahalla. The door to the inside of the compound was wide open. This was a worry – who was in the compound. Walk back to the car and driver, wherever they were now, skirting dodgy again. Stand in the street and call for help. Go to my office. Tough choice.

It seemed quiet in the compound. I ran across the car park to my office block. Sprinted up the stairs. Unlocked my office. Locked myself in. Sat down. Breathe. I needed to go to the toilet – well you would, wouldn't you. I ran down the corridor, locked myself in a cubicle. No water, no flush. Back to the office. I switched my desktop on. No power. I started up my laptop. No internet.

The next compound, the other side of the wall, was a church. The singing started. It was quite pleasant, but it was deafening. I nearly didn't hear my phone.

"Are you coming to the pub". "Oh yes, come get me". No wahalla there.

HEIGHT, SIGHT AND GIBBERISH

I was invited back to Moscow for my last work permit medical. But not Doctor Digit. This time I was going to an international and highly reputable clinic. I had to wait a few days, because they were moving across Moscow from one building to another. Expanding by all accounts. So, a few days later I turned up, wondering what this year's medical had in store for me. Oh the anticipation.

I was shown into the doctor. He was French. He was part of the clinic's expansion, was in Russia for the first time and had been there two days. He was also quite short – maybe 5 feet 6 inches. He apologized that his office was full of boxes. All part of the move apparently.

Weight. He found the scales and weighed me. 92kg. One of

the few pieces of equipment that was set up, was one of those measuring tapes mounted high up on the wall, that you pull down until it touches the top of your head, and you read how tall you are in the plastic window. I stood under it, and with difficulty the Doctor reached up to grasp the tape. He pulled it down to touch my head. "5 feet 11 inches", he said. "I've been 6 feet one inch for the last twenty years", I said. We had a bit of discussion. He checked again. Presumably in case I'd grown since he measured me five minutes before. 5 feet eleven.

To prove a point, and for good measure – sorry, I got him to stand against the wall. I said, "you are 5 feet 4 inches". I've never seen a man so indignant. You'd think I'd insulted his manhood. The French do indignant really well. "I am 5 feet 6 inches !!!!", as though it was some sort of Anglo-French conspiracy. Tape measure was mounted on the wall. But at the wrong height. We agreed on 6 feet 1. It was going to be a long day.

Then we did the numbers in the couloured dots colour blindness test. I read the numbers. I'm not colour blind. He said he trusted me. In fact, he said he had to trust me because he was green and red colour blind.

Then we did the reading eyesight test. A plasticized page, with text repeated three times. In large font at the top, medium font in the middle and tiny font at the bottom. It was an international clinic, dealing with the whole range of nationalities that worked in Moscow. They had the text in every imaginable language. Except English. I helped him search through some boxes, but we couldn't find the English version. And except French. I speak French, so I offered to read the French version. But we couldn't find that either. We did find the Russian version. Just as well because I was running out of languages.

The Chinese version looked tricky even in the big font.

I read him the Russian version, reading the very big font, the medium font and then the small font. Usually the testers stop you after a sentence or two. But he didn't tell me to stop, so I read the whole thing, whilst he listened intently. It must have looked like dad reading his child a story. I felt like tucking him in. When I finished, he didn't say anything immediately. So, I said that if I'd made mistakes, it was because my Russian wasn't perfect, not because of my eyesight.

He was hesitating because he didn't speak Russian. Not one word. So, he had no idea what I'd said. I could have been speaking badger. Or Urdu. Still it was all so much better than an invitation to Doctor Digit.

I could have been speaking badger.

CHAPTER THIRTEEN

Beer, Busses and Balls Of Fire

IN THESE REMOTE places, food takes on an importance out of proportion to its nutritional value. Everyone has an opinion. Nationalities, cultures and religions have different preferences, prejudices and limitations. And no one is ever happy all the time. You are lucky if anyone is happy any of the time.

... Fifers, Teessiders, Scousers or Glaswegians ...

Oilfields now, everywhere, ban alcohol – but that wasn't always the case. A lot of the people attracted by the oilfield in the 70s, 80s and 90s came out of the UK heavy industries – mining, shipbuilding, chemicals – they were characters, and characters generally like a drink. If they weren't Fifers, Teessiders, Scousers or Glaswegians, they were farmers from Friesland or Texans – mostly with a red neck. They're characters, and drinkers, too.

In Aberdeen airport, in the 80s, the bar was at the end of the terminal building. Access to the bar was cunningly blocked by the one long luggage belt – it ran right across the bar entrance. When we got back from offshore, some of the guys wouldn't bother getting their bag. They would climb onto the luggage belt, into the middle bit, up onto the other side of the belt, off the other side and up to the bar. It saved ten metres or so. No time to waste. And they would be there long after the belt stopped, and long after the last train home left from Aberdeen station.

A few people could be a little shakey at the beginning of an offshore trip. And there is no truth in the rumour that my shift bought a calculator with especially big buttons. For anyone that needed it in the first few days. Platforms offshore were genuinely alcohol free. But at Xmas and New Year, everyone got two cans of beer each as a concession. The Xmas before I went offshore, there'd been an accident and a small explosion on one platform. No one was hurt, and alcohol didn't play a part in the incident. However, in responding to the incident, a few senior platform staff couldn't be found. They weren't constrained by the two cans of beer per person rule, and rumour had it they couldn't be found for a reason.

As a result, the first Xmas I was offshore, was the first Xmas with no concessions. So I was used to the strictest of regimes. When I went to a work camp, in the middle of the Omani desert – an Islamic country – and found a fully legal bar, I thought it really was Xmas. The bar sold everything you could imagine. Fosters and Boddingtons were the beers of choice. We had a couple of full time Indian barmen and it was open every night from 6 until 11. Later, on special occasions. The guys were still complaining because a few months before, they had stopped opening at lunchtime. A different world.

There was never a single problem in the bar or related to alcohol or with getting people to work the next day. The only problem was that you signed for what you bought, and your bar bill came straight off your salary. A few people had a consumption that was challenging their salary.

The answer was homebrew. We all lived in a camp environment in bachelor rooms. P block became the home brewers' accommodation of choice. All the bad boys were already there. Suddenly everyone wanted to move in. The fixings were brought back from Europe after leave. The equipment was begged or borrowed from the laboratory. Sugar was begged or borrowed from the catering contractor. And empty Grolsch bottles – those nice beer bottles with the wire cage spring bungs – were redirected from the bar refuse.

The etiquette was to wait for an invitation for a night out at P block. The beer was good, and it wasn't long before mass production kicked in. And, the best bit, it didn't come off your salary. P block became a regular haunt for the next couple of years. I didn't do the brewing, just the drinking. In Ramadan, the official bar shut for a month, and P block took on a whole new importance. However, all good things come to an end, and at a certain point, a complaint was made to a higher authority that P block was in full flow during Ramadan. So, we had no alternative but to cease trading.

We were given a couple of days grace to dispose of all the evidence before we'd be in deep shit. Lose your work permit type shit. I didn't live in P block, I was just a shareholder. Some of the guys were on leave, so we had to break into their rooms and clear them out. There was a hundred gallons brewing in one room, so with hindsight, I suppose it was a bit out of hand. And that was only one room. We poured the brew down every available drain, toilet, shower, sink and washbasin. There were five or six of us working in full panic mode. It still took all day. There was so much that beer froth started appearing in every road drain, toilet, shower, sink and washbasin in the camp. The distinctive smell of brewing hung over P block for a week. All the drains went to a septic tank system. The alcohol killed all the bugs in the water treatment plant, and the septic tank system had to be pumped out and restarted.

But the biggest job was getting rid of all the jars, buckets, jugs and bottles. There were thousands. This involved giving an Indian bulldozer driver a small present to bulldoze a big hole in the desert in the middle of the night. In a couple of centuries its going to confuse an archaeologist.

The price of real estate in P block crashed. We were all back in the bar. Handing over chunks of salary.

The price of real estate in P block crashed.

In Gabon there was a shop. Only one and it was smaller than an average off license. It was the only source of food and drink for a hundred expatriate families. It was run by a contractor who must have been incentivized to carry no stock and charge the highest number of zeroes that you could programme into a till. There was a range of twenty different types of olives, but for a week we had no potatoes, no rice and no toilet roll. Regab was the beer of choice. I had a theory – after a lot of research - that the green bottles gave you hangovers and the brown bottles didn't. Every few bottles would stink of hypochlorite – the bottle sterilizing solution.

Chickens featured regularly in that part of West Africa. Apart from Dinner the chicken – remember him - the staple food there was chicken and rice. It was always chicken wings; I never saw a chicken breast. Did they breed special octopus, breastless chickens? Star beer was the beer of choice in that area in case you were wondering – the same green and brown bottles as Regab, with the same occasional slug of hypochlorite. Occasionally, if I fancied a change, I'd go wild and have rice and chicken.

Food was a challenge in Russia too – as you will read in a minute. I visited one drilling rig in winter and they had solved the quantity issue, if not the variety issue. They'd obviously brought in several hundred frozen chickens. Complete – not just the legs. But faced with the problem of not having freezer space for a few weeks' worth of frozen chicken, and the fact it was minus thirty outside, they just stacked the frozen chickens up outside the kitchen. A bit like some people stack wood. Top marks for innovation, but you wouldn't want to eat it.

In Gabon, the French culture shone through. Even in the oilfield, there was half a litre of wine with dinner for everyone – built into the catering contract. We had a bar in the oilfield too – it had been a wooden log hut – called a paillotte, with a straw roof. Then to help people stop catching malaria, it had been fitted with Perspex windows. The bar was open from 6 until 8:30 each evening and sold wine and beer only. There was never any trouble here either.

That said, every once in a while, if European bands or singers came to work the few hotels in Gabon, we'd fly them in, share the cost, and they'd do their act in the paillotte. Let's just say, not many well known acts have played the paillotte. We had a strange combination of acts at times. We had a local

Not many well known acts have played the paillotte.

dance troupe come and do local dances. It was all going well. Then they started swinging flaming balls of straw around on ropes. The flames were inches from the straw roof. My heart was in my mouth. The fire crew were oblivious - cheering and clapping louder than most. So maybe I was just a worrier. We had a young Dutch group come. There was an attractive young blonde singer. That was going well too – she sang, "voulez-vous couchez avec moi" to the appreciative French speaking Gabonese crowd …. they asked for it again. And again, and again. Not sure if she spoke French or not. Either way, I went looking for Fabrice, the head of security. I found him – he was singing along with more enthusiasm than I'd ever seen him muster before. I went to bed. It was all too much of a worry.

Russia has a strange relationship with alcohol. In the early 2000s, every time I visited, I'd be met at the airplane door by an interpreter – you needed one just to get through passport control. The interpreters we used at that time, were all men in their fifties, who'd learnt English in the military. They'd never spent time in an English-speaking country. In general they just weren't much good.

One interpreter, who translated for me on several trips, was a gargantuan bloke. It was cold in winter, so in addition to his enormous frame, he would wear a big fur hat and a voluminous coat. The hat looked like he had an Alsation balanced on his head. When I was having a conversation with someone, we would stand opposite each other, and Sergey would stand to one side to translate – like the tennis umpire. As the conversation progressed, he got excited, and maybe a bit flustered and he had this habit of gradually moving between me, and the person I was trying to speak to. He was so big, that at a certain point I could no longer see anything except his coat and hat. I'd be trying to peer round him, or jump up and down, to catch a glimpse of my conversation partner.

Sergey taught me a lot about drinking in Russia. I was meeting prospective suppliers, contractors, partners and local officials. Meetings would often include lunch. It was customary in the restaurants in Siberia, that at lunch a half bottle of Vodka would be served. A half bottle at every place setting. For lunch.

I noticed that Sergey would say a few words to the waiter, and his half bottle would be taken away. And everyone accepted that. It wasn't socially acceptable in this culture to just flat out refuse to drink. That immediately destroyed trust. But Sergey got away with it – I was keen to learn how. I asked him. He said, "I'm a recovering alcoholic – I tell the waiter – everyone understands". From then on, if I wanted to avoid drinking, I had a dilemma – upset my hosts by refusing to drink with them or tell them all I was a recovering alcoholic. I could never decide which was the most socially acceptable.

There is a Russian anecdote. "Vodka without beer is like money in the wind". For a serious session, the Russians drink vodka shots with a litre of Baltica 10 chaser. Baltica used to be the Russian beer of choice in case you needed to know. However, if you find yourself in this position, and wonder why you can't stand, and your Russian host is fresh as a daisy, there are likely to be two reasons. One. He, or less likely she, has been practicing diligently since birth as well as having a genetic disposition to not getting pissed. Two. He had a few large gulps of beer to make a decent space in his glass. Then when he took his Vodka shot in one along with you, he went straight for the beer glass along with you. But while you have ever bigger glugs of strong beer, he spits his Vodka into the space in his beer glass – never swallowing Vodka, or anything of what becomes a cocktail of vodka and beer. You've been warned. Or acquired a new skill. As you wish.

Remember we went to Kamchatka skiing. And us three Brits struggled to keep up with the Germans, Austrians and Swiss. We were way second in the skiing. But we were outright winners in the Russian traditional drinking competition. They did look poorly. Sorry fellas.

There were no amenities in Ahwaz in Iran. A city, at that time, of a million and a half Persians and 3 Westerners. Including me. One Friday, my interpreter told me there was a pizza restaurant. Iranian food is great, but after a couple of weeks, the possibility of pizza was too much. I just had to know what Iranian pizza was like. So, we went there for lunch. The Iranian people in general were very welcoming to me. There were a dozen people in there as I sat down with my interpreter – they looked at the foreigner, but they were all smiling in my general direction. We ordered and waited.

Friday prayers had just finished ...

A few minutes later, the Imam from the nearby mosque arrived for a pizza lunch too. Possibly not a traditional Friday lunch. He had a small entourage. It was Friday and Friday prayers had just finished. My interpreter explained all of this, in hushed tones and with a worried expression. The mood changed, the atmosphere went cold, the looks in my direction increased and were no longer friendly. "We need to leave", the interpreter told me. So, we did. Pronto. I never did test Iranian pizza. And I never did find the Iranian beer of choice.

At a certain point we installed an electronic card access system in Siberia. It got you access through the main gate into the field. Got you access to offices and industrial areas where you needed access, and stopped you going where you weren't supposed to. It also allowed you to be fed. No card authorization, no food. With a field the size of Wales, it could be difficult to get to see people. Also, true that on occasion, people would avoid me. Until the end of their shift, then they'd escape the field, and it would be another month before I could see the whites of their eyes. This was when I found the most pleasing use of the electronic card system. I'd stop their meal authorization and they wouldn't get fed. Not even the most difficult cases lasted more than a couple of days before they got hungry and turned up in my office.

Back in Iran, Friday afternoons were a bit tricky in Ahwaz in general. I'd been out with driver and interpreter to look at a piece of land as a potential site. On the way back into Ahwaz, we turned a corner between bombed out buildings, and were straight into the back of a large, excited crowd. They were cheering and chanting. A large and excited crowd, if you are tolerated but not really welcome, is usually bad news. Fortunately, the driver, who really did look after me, managed to back us out of the crowd. We later learned that that location was that Friday's spot for a bit of public punishment. I'd been lucky not to join a stoning. Or worse.

I went to Mumbai to interview technicians for Oman. There had been a failed recruitment campaign a few months before. It had failed for a few reasons. Top of the list of reasons, was that it had frequently been a different guy who had passed the interview, than had got off the plane in Oman to start work. For a fee, you could get a professional interviewee to get the job. Then your only problem was that you couldn't actually do the job.

We also needed the technicians to drive big four-wheel drive vehicles several hours across the desert on a regular basis. But when the applicant said they could drive, they meant they had an Indian driving license. Generally that meant they could drive the three-wheel, three gear, maximum 20 mph, Tuk Tuks. When faced with a Landcruiser and a desert, the problem appeared, and the driver disappeared.

So, this time they sent me to recruit.

First job was to take a photo, so we could match the interviewee with the future employee. I had a hire Landcruiser. Second job was to do a driving test. In most cases, we got no further than a few hundred metres, and I drove back. Next.

In one memorable interview, I stopped the conversation after twenty minutes or so. The candidate had picked his nose constantly through the photo taking, the driving test and the interview. He'd made an impression alright. At least two knuckles up there at all times. I just couldn't take him back to join my team.

... two knuckles up there at all times.

Recruitment hadn't gone well, so the Pakistani agent who had done the advertising and searching said he'd take me for dinner. He said we'd go to the best Pakistani restaurant in Mumbai. I'd gone on this trip with half a suitcase full of food, so I didn't need to eat anything local. And the other half of the suitcase was full of medicine in case I did. But he persuaded me,

I said yes, and I was genuinely looking forward to a night out.

We arrived and studied a menu. The agent was a wise old head. After a couple of minutes, he said, "don't have any fish". That ruled out half the menu and seemed a bit direct. "It's been hot, and the fridge is broken". I'm not a fussy eater, but my appetite wavered a bit. I had lamb. The whole bill, at the best Pakistani restaurant in Mumbai, came to 4 dollars. Whilst appreciating the thought, I didn't think the agent had challenged his expense account too much. I'd found out what I was worth.

We had the first case of drunk at work in Russia in my first week. I couldn't figure out the employment law, so had no idea what sanction I could apply. So, I stopped trying. I just took away the pass to my field. I could do that.

We had a room near the gate where we did induction training with anyone new to the field. There were no data privacy laws in Russia. So, I put the confiscated gate pass on the wall of the training room. In further weeks and months and years, as we detected alcohol, the gate pass would be confiscated and would be pinned on the wall too. The confiscated passes would be shown during induction training. I expected this to be a great deterrent in a world where people valued good employment. I expected that word would get round that we had zero tolerance, and after a few months people would comply with our genuinely zero alcohol policy. In my last week, after six years, we pinned the 584th pass on the wall. I'd made absolutely no difference to the culture at all.

I like a beer. So, with my own staff I made a concession. At the end of their 28-day shift, people would travel home by train in summer. Every train had a buffet. And the first stop for them, and me, was the buffet for a beer. After 28 days of stress and hard work, I would head straight to the buffet, determined to drink it dry. I'd manage two small bottles and collapse in an exhausted heap.

In the winter, the trains became unreliable. So, we ran coaches to the main cities. The coaches didn't have buffets. There became a custom and practice, that passengers would get the driver to stop at the first roadside kiosk and buy crates of beer and bottles of vodka. They were delaying the bus. They were wandering around at the side of a busy road, making a nuisance of themselves, half pissed.

No Yorkshireman in history has ever volunteered to buy that much beer.

I thought I'd kill two birds with one stone. As a thank you for a month of hard graft, the company would buy two bottles of beer for each coach passenger. No more delaying the bus, no more hanging around at the side of the road. No more spirits. No Yorkshireman in history has ever volunteered to buy that much beer. An inspired idea in my mind.

Some of the Russians counselled me. "They won't understand what you are trying to do Chris – it's a big mistake". But how much trouble can anyone get into on two bottles of beer. Had to be a winner.

We ran coaches on Monday, Wednesday and Friday. We started with free beer on the Monday. I was travelling on the Friday. I was looking forward to my company sponsored two bottles of beer.

After the Monday trip I got reports of bad behaviour on the bus. And the bus company complained. I persevered.

After the Wednesday trip, the driver formally complained – by all accounts a small group had consumed all the beer, given the driver grief. The bus company complained. My staff complained. The road police complained. So, I had to stop it. We hadn't even got as far as Friday.

I never had that company sponsored beer.

AN AUDIENCE WITH AN APPLE PIE

The very first time I went to Siberia, I was sent on a specific mission. I got a briefing as I passed through the main office in Moscow. "We're fairly sure there are three oil wells and a small camp with some people still there. But nobody's been there for years, so we're not sure what you'll find". "Figure out what we'd have to do with the camp to move in, say 250 people, just to start".

There was a camp with about twelve people living in it. There were a few operators for the three oil wells. Anywhere you have people you need a medic – so there was a doctor. And you have to transport people, so there were two drivers. When you've got ten people or so, you need someone to do laundry, clean and cook. And someone to maintain the camp, and at least one electrician. And when you get up to that many people you need a boss. And with that lot, you need a bigger camp.

It's a self-fulfilling prophecy. Three people producing oil, ten people looking after them. The two old ladies who did the cooking, lived in the village and travelled out every day. They bought the food in the village shop. Which was amazing, because there wasn't one. It was a case of what they could get, which sometimes wasn't much and sometimes wasn't anything. Not their fault. But the food was shockingly, gut churningly, bad.

Travelling back to Europe through the Moscow office, I presented what needed to be done with the camp to accommodate 250 people. And the last words I said, were something like, "Oh and we'd need to upgrade the kitchen and food supply, or we'd all be getting scurvy". Characteristically flippant, but making a point.

... or we'd all be getting scurvy.

A few months later, I had to go back to the field. It was a specific job this time – environmental surveys. I passed through the Moscow office again for my briefing. As I was leaving, someone mentioned to me, that I should buy some chocolates. And give them to the two cooks. My flippant comments had got back to the ladies, had been felt as personal criticism and hadn't gone down well. These ladies would be feeding me for the next couple of weeks. I went to buy some chocolates.

The boss of the camp, in an oilfield, is imaginatively called, the camp boss. The camp boss was Vitali. Not to be confused with Vitaly the mayor. Camp boss Vitali was a gentleman, became a good friend and still is to this day. He spoke no English. He welcomed me as I arrived late one night. Trying to speak through the vast bulk of Sergey, he explained that because I was coming, the ladies had managed to get some special food. I was instantly embarrassed. But quietly delighted.

I got up the next morning and went for breakfast. I was feverish with anticipation as to what the special food could be. I was also very hungry. The special food arrived. It was pizza. Not a traditional breakfast. But also not the whole story apparently, there was more. Ice cream. I ate it of course – anything else would have been rude. And thanked the ladies profusely.

After a day's work, I went for dinner. I couldn't wait to see what was for dinner. It was pizza. And ice cream. It went on like this for a week. The whole camp was having pizza and ice cream for breakfast and dinner every day, to please me. What could you say?

On Sunday morning, after a pizza and ice cream breakfast, Vitali took me to one side. In a whisper, looking around in case anyone was listening, he gave me some critical news. The ladies had managed to get everything needed for us to have … apple pie. With unreasonable excitement, I thanked him and went off to work, already looking forward to dinner. I did wonder what we'd been missing – the apples or the flour. Anyway, it would be different. And not ice cream.

Dinner came. Pizza was had. The eyes of fifteen people were trained on the old lady who had been doing apple pie. And instead of ice cream, apple pie appeared and was presented on the table in front of me. It was slightly bigger than the Mr. Kipling variety – the ones that come in packs of six. Except in this case, there weren't six. There was one.

We did a sterling job, dividing Mr. Kipling into fifteen portions, whilst hiding disappointment, and not laughing.

… dividing Mr. Kipling into fifteen portions …

All the while being watched by fourteen people who are sick of pizza and ice cream. My crumbs were delicious. My sliver of apple was tasty. I made a note to mention this in the Moscow office, on my way back to Europe. But I didn't know what I was going to say this time.

CHAPTER FOURTEEN

Filters, Fines
(and Some More Fines)

I GENERALLY HAVE more luck with cars than planes. But not always.

In Oman we had a Suzuki Vitara. You needed a four-wheel drive to go to the few shops there were. And Ruwi high street. You had to get out and lock the front wheel hubs manually. It wasn't hi-tec. It wasn't comfortable. But it never, ever got stuck and it never, ever broke down. And we certainly battered it.

Jebel Sham is a 10,000-foot mountain, and with care you could get all the way to the top by 4WD on rocky tracks. We went one weekend in the Vitara. Totally pleased with ourselves for getting there despite the toughest track I'd ever seen, we set up camp and put the kettle on for a brew. An hour later a Toyota Corolla appeared – it was orange and white – the uniform at the time for a taxi. In fairness, it was struggling with a particularly big rocky step. The taxi driver backed up to be able to take a run-up, gunned the engine, bounced up the step and kept going. Most likely the passenger was a bedou out looking for his goats.

... a bedou out looking for his goats.

There was a consignment of Land Rover Discoveries en route to Iraq when the Gulf War broke out. The ship diverted to Muscat. A couple of hundred Discoveries were unloaded on the dockside – all the same version, all the same colour – the most basic spec. They stood on the dockside in the Middle East heat for about a year and were then sold. Cheap. But with a warranty. We bought one, as did most of my colleagues at work.

I worked in the desert for a week, then had a week off at the coast. Newly arrived for a week at work, we'd swap Discovery stories from the week off before. I'd find out what had broken on everyone else's Discovery. I'd tell everyone what had broken on mine. Then I'd go home for a week off and check my own car. Sure enough, if it hadn't already broken on your own Discovery, it was about to. Every rubber, plastic or elastomeric cmponent failed. Fuel pumps, shock absorbers and steering racks were next. Only one person persuaded the dealer to take his Discovery back – it was that bad. The dealer came to collect it. It had a flat tyre. The dealer got the hydraulic jack out to change the tyre. The seal in the jack burst and spewed hydraulic oil everywhere. Discoveries at their best.

We lived at the top of a steep hill. We'd been in Europe on leave. I'd come back to work and my family had stayed for a few more weeks. All the flights from Europe arrived in the evening - I took the Discovery to the airport to pick them up. Driving home, the Discovery, full of family and luggage, broke down. I gave it a good kicking and then did what every Discovery owner did - I hitched the last two- or three-kilometers home to get the Vitara. Somewhere I have a photo of a new Discovery, full of luggage, being towed up the steep hill by a beat up old

Vitara. Here's hoping someone from LandRover buys this book. I'd sell them the photo, or destroy it, for a price.

I had a Toyota Landcruiser in Russia. It never missed a beat. But one slack afternoon, we did do comparison tests with the local built Lada four-wheel drives. On serious snow, the Lada's have a much better stopping distance. The tyres are so small, cheap and narrow that they just dig into the snow in a few metres. You never know when that knowledge will come in handy. Here's hoping someone from Lada buys this book.

The only time the Landcruisers were a problem, was when it got cold. Minus 50 degrees centigrade cold. Down to a certain temperature you just plug in a factory fitted electric blanket that sits round the engine – and it starts no problem. Below about minus 25, you leave the engine running 24 hours a day. When it gets down to minus 40 or so, the hydraulic oil in the clutch gets thick, and you can't physically push the clutch down unless you've got Chris Hoy's thighs. If you get the clutch down, the gearbox oil is so thick, you can't get it into gear. At minus 50, if you get it into gear, the tyres have frozen with a flat spot at the bottom – so for the first ten kilometers your head bounces off the roof once every time the wheels go round. It's like sitting on a sewing machine needle.

Gabon was massively expensive. With a hundred expatriate families – if someone was leaving, then you could come to a deal and buy their car. If no one was leaving, then you had no option but to buy a new one. There were no dealers or show-rooms in the village where we lived, so it meant flying up to the nearest city. You had to have a four-wheel drive because there were 10 kilometers of road, and then you ran out. There were only two options – Mitsubishi and Toyota. There were only two models – long wheelbase and short wheelbase. There were only two prices – outrageous and extortionate. With that kind of choice, the dealers didn't actually bother to keep cars to look at or drive. The showroom was an empty building with a desk where you paid through the nose.

There were only two prices – outrageous and extortionate.

There were no roads into the area where we lived. Your new car had to come on a barge by sea. The barge sailed once a week and it took two days and nights. The first time you saw your brand new vastly expensive car, was when someone drove it from the barge jetty to your house. I only know of one that ended up in the river. Mine arrived – it had dents across the whole roof where it had been locked down onto the barge with chains and no padding. It had six inches of seawater in the footwells – the driver's window had been left down for the two-day trip and it had been rough. Still, if it arrived a bit battered, it just saved a few weeks – after a few weeks of driving through the bush it would be battered anyway.

I don't think Mitsubishi knew that they had any cars in Gabon. The cars were obviously fitted out locally. The front seats were Mitsubishi's, but the back seats were benches mounted on steel channel and bolted in. The windscreen and front windows were Mitsubishi's, but all the rear windows were locally cut and fitted Perspex – they mostly fitted, except where they didn't. They scratched so you couldn't see through them within weeks – you could see through the gaps round the edges where they didn't quite fit though. Here's hoping someone from Mitsubishi buys this book.

We had friends who spent a small fortune on a new long wheel-base Landcruiser. It got off the barge a bit battered, but nothing unusual. Within a few days, they'd hit a rock and it had fractured a pipe carrying hydraulic oil to the front brakes. No chance of getting spares, so they just plugged off the broken pipe, and drove round with only back brakes, for the next year or so. People bought spares when they went to Europe on leave, so a year later they bought some bits for the front brake pipes in Liverpool. People brought tyres back from Europe in their suitcase.

I needed an oil filter. I noted the serial number like a good engineer, and when I was in the UK on leave, I spent a happy hour with the man with the books, in Halfords. Serial number didn't exist. No such oil filter. Had to wait another six months to try again. This time I took the oil filter itself to Europe with me in my hand luggage. Another happy hour in Halfords, and I came out with half a dozen filters identical to the old one. They fitted ok but were supposed to be for the engine on a Seat van. They weren't supposed to fit any Mitsubishi that Mitsubishi would admit to building. The engines obviously got finished and fitted locally too.

I've had a couple of speeding fines. Three points in the UK – I paid the fine and took the points. On holiday in Iceland, I was taking advantage of good weather and a clear road. There were hundreds of kilometers between settlements. So, I was doing a hundred or so, in an area with an 80 limit. Kilometers that is. Guilty. A police car coming the other way, with a radar camera facing forwards, pulled me over.

Iceland was unbelievably expensive at that time. 20 dollars equivalent for a can of coke or a petrol station hotdog. You just had to stop reading the numbers and forget the exchange rate, otherwise it would spoil your day.

Sitting in the back of the police car. "Do you know how fast you were going?". "About 85 I think". They showed me the radar photo – I'd been doing 105. "Do you know what the speed limit is?" "It's a hundred I think". It had been 80. I did know that. "You'll have to go to the police station in Xdfegyhu village to pay your fine". Xdfegyhu was hundreds of kilometers in the wrong direction. My face collapsed. "Or you can pay us now", as they got out one of those old fashioned swipey mechanical credit card machines. "I'll pay you now", I brightened up – then the inner Yorkshireman remembered how expensive this was going to be. "That will be 2500 Krona". It sounded a lot; my face collapsed a bit more as I started converting it into pounds. It was about 15 quid. I must have made a mistake. "Are you sure?". They were sure. I couldn't help but say, "that's remarkably good value". They thought it was funny – just as well.

"that's remarkably good value"

I thought about asking if it was that price every day and no matter what speed you were doing. Given the distances in Iceland, it would have been worth it. I suppose I might have been pushing my luck. So, I didn't.

We had the Mitsubishi Pajero in Gabon. At work in the oilfield, I had an old LandRover Defender. We had a fleet of old Defenders throughout the field. The roads were made of laterite – a dark red dust. If it mixed with water, it was very acidic. And the whole place was in a tropical rain forest. So, there was definitely water. The Defenders rotted. We had a constant industry going on rebuilding Defenders. I inherited the newest and best Defender in the field from my predecessor – it had air conditioning, a floor without holes, wheels that stayed on, and everything. It was the only car with air conditioning. It was hot, and without air conditioning, with windows open, the cars were always full of laterite dust.

Every time someone senior came to the field; they'd want to borrow a car. They'd usually only come to see me, so they felt entitled to borrow my car. So senior visitors, including the bean counters, saw the only good car in good condition. They didn't realise the battered old, wrecks everyone else was driving round in, so they kept counting the beans. Some of the technical guys had delicate electronic equipment, tools and spares. These were all knackered by the heat and the laterite dust. I killed two birds with one stone.

I gave my car, to the technical guys with the most need. We shuffled cars around, so that deliberately I had the worst car. The one that was actually six or seven cars welded together, that broke down every day, where you sweated buckets and choked on dust. So the visiting bean counters got a different experience. Wasn't long before we got enough beans to get a new fleet of Toyotas. And I got enough kudos from the boys to last me a few lifetimes.

But in the meantime, the CEO came to visit. Might have been coincidence, but on this occasion, he decided to drive to the field. There were no roads to get there, but if you took two days, and arranged two landing craft to take you across two lagoon systems, it was just possible. He had a new LandRover Discovery as his company car. I wonder if the bloke from LandRover is still reading. The CEO broke down somewhere between lagoon systems, and after a few hours someone managed to get him going again. He broke down again a couple of hours away from the field, and we rescued him.

He decided that I needed to replace the knackered old Defender I had given myself. He was sick of his Discovery. He killed two birds with one stone. He gave me his Discovery, flew out of the field rather than drive back, and no doubt ordered himself something new and shiny to replace the Discovery. Now I had a new Discovery that broke down on a regular basis. Just like old times.

... bright orange golf umbrella above the sunroof ...

It had another fault as well. It had one of the early slide and tilt sunroofs. Maybe that had been fitted locally because it didn't. Fit that is. It rained a lot, and every time it rained, the front seats, passenger, and me, got wet. To stop people killing themselves too regularly we had a 40-kilometer speed limit. We had a few goes at fixing the sunroof. We stopped short at welding a plate in. We did try sealing it permanently. But we failed. So, I took to driving around with a bright orange golf umbrella above the sunroof, with the handle lashed to the centre console. It satisfied my love of the eccentric. It's the first time I'd found golf useful. And I was easily spotted.

The bean counters would ask about the umberella, and I'd tell them. It didn't hurt to keep reminding the boys with long trousers and the purse strings that we still needed that new fleet of Toyotas.

Every once in a while, I forgot the umbrella. Called out at three in the morning to an emergency. I drove to the problem

– it wasn't raining, but it had been chucking it down all night. My seat was wet of course. I pulled up at the emergency site, picked my helmet up off the passenger seat where I'd left it, and put it on my head. It was full of water.

Three in the morning, looking at something on fire, backside wet, feet already wet because of the rubbish boots we had, drenched from my helmet acting as a bucket. I wasn't laughing.

En route from Russia to the UK, I'd gone to the North of Holland – Friesland - on business for a few days. I'd hired a car at Amsterdam airport and driven North. At the end of the few days business, I drove back to Amsterdam, to catch the flight for some well-earned leave. I was late, the traffic was bad, and I didn't want to miss the flight. And I didn't. But a week later, I got the speeding fine.

You used to pay bills in Holland using an acceptogiro. It was a preprinted piece of card, with all the information on it – you added your bank account number, signed it, gave it to the bank and the bill got paid. I'd got an acceptgiro for my speeding fine. The fine doubled if I was late paying. And doubled again. And again. Without a Dutch bank account, I couldn't figure out how to pay it.

I was going back to Russia a few weeks later, through Amsterdam airport, with 2 hours between planes. There was an ABN bank in the terminal. That was the answer. Arriving at the airport I went straight to the ABN bank. "No, you can't pay that here because you don't have an account with us". "But you could pay it at Spaarbank". "Where's the nearest Spaarbank?", assuming there was one in the terminal somewhere. "Central Amsterdam, get a train and a couple of trams …". Thanks.

With two hours, that wasn't going to work.

I arrived back in Siberia with an unpaid acceptogiro, no plan to pay it, and no opportunity for the next four weeks. By that time it would be a gazillion Euros – a number to offend anyone genetically Yorkshire. I was telling one of the Dutch guys – Jan - my troubles, when he said he could pay it online for me if I gave him the cash. Unusual for the Dutch to be so helpful, so I bit his hand off. I gave him the money and off he went.

... the people who made shit happen, and dealt with the shit when it did.

The next morning, I had my daily Operations meeting. This is where we explained how little we'd achieved the day before, calamities occurred and impending, and overpromised how much we planned to do that day. As well as a bit of a rant where required. It was a serious conversation between the people who made shit happen, and dealt with the shit when it did.

Apart from running a team of several hundred engineers and technicians, and keeping 500 oil wells healthy, dealing with my Dutch speeding fines and generally being a social asset, Jan had a bread machine in his office, so was chief baker. And very popular. I promoted a casual meeting with this bunch – we were under enough stress, in a difficult enough place – generally I preferred to wear carpet slippers, and to munch some of Jan's fresh toast, in between listening to the team.

Round the table to ask my ten or so direct reports, if there'd been any safety issues or concerns or successes. I got to Jan. His face lit up. "I'd just like to say that I've paid the Field Managers speeding fine" and gave me the receipt. Only me not in on the joke, and the place erupted. I liked Jan.

SATURDAY AND THE SLINKY

I had a driver in West Africa - Joseph. Sounds grand, but no foreigner would want to take the risk of driving themselves in that area, so it wasn't grand. It was coming up to the Rugby World Cup in 2001. No chance of getting Rugby on local TV, so I took a shortwave radio back there with me after leave.

I normally worked Saturdays and Sundays. The first game was on a Saturday afternoon. In anticipation, I tested radio reception in my office. Rubbish. But I had a plan. I sent Joseph into town to buy me 25 feet of light two core cable. Then he got it soldered on one end onto a 3.5mm jack plug and soldered at the other end onto two crocodile clips. Half an hour later he was back – unusually, job done.

I worked in a satellite office, away from the main office. The office compound was surrounded by a ten-foot concrete block wall. There was a guard post and a locked gate. My office was on the first floor, with an office window that looked out onto the wall – maybe 5 metres from window to wall. I was about as far away from the gate and guard post as you could get.

The wall round the perimeter of the compound was probably 200m in total. It was topped with a coil of razor wire. The razor wire was held on top of the wall by lumps of cement at seemingly random intervals.

Saturday came along, and the rugby was imminent. I was in the office with the radio on listening to the world service – they were doing commentary live. An hour before kickoff I gave Joseph a shout. "Go outside my office window - when I give you the two crocodile clips, climb up and clip them to the razor wire on top of the wall." This responsibility wasn't exactly specified in his job description. I directed clipping from my office window whilst Joseph tottered about on the razor wire.

Crocodile clips attached, I put the jack plug into the external aerial socket of my radio. The reception was perfect. The razor wire coil must have been just the right length. I was dead chuffed. No one else in the office, so I ramped up the volume as I worked away. Kick off came and it was great being able to listen to England playing whoever it was.

... attached to the biggest lightning conductor in West Africa.

Somewhere in the first half, a bit of a thunderstorm started in the distance. By half time it was violent, closer and raining heavily. As the second half started, I got a bit worried that I was attached to the biggest lightening conductor in West Africa. The sky and the office were black, but the lightning flashes were frequent and blinding. Reluctantly, I decided I'd better unplug myself.

No sign of Joseph – he was hunkered down somewhere – avoiding any job, and any delicate adjustment of my aerial. No way I was going out in that rain to fiddle about with razor wire. From inside my office window I gave my cable a gentle tug. Those crocodile clips were strong. I gave it a bit more of a pull. Eventually I gave it a really good yank. And I watched as the cable pulled the razor wire off the top of the wall. I rushed up to the window. In both directions, the razor wire was rolling itself off the top of the wall. It was a giant slinky.

Only this slinky didn't roll down to the next step of the stairs, watched by an amused child. Instead this one rolled off onto the cars of my fellow Saturday workers, reverse parked against the wall. I was standing at the window like a stunned mullet – mouth open, no words coming out.

Of course, I came clean and owned up to my misdemeanor. Did I hell. I found Joseph, bought his silence, retrieved the cable, scarpered to the pub and missed the second half.

YOU KNOW WHERE THIS IS

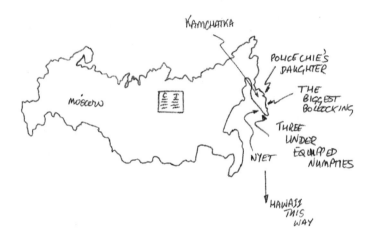

AND THIS IS AFRICA AGAIN

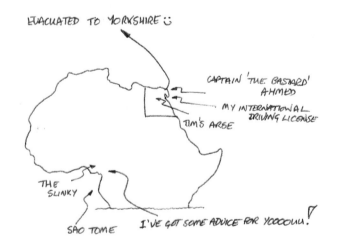

CHAPTER FIFTEEN

Adjectives, Advice and Captain Ahmed

I WAS DOING alright learning Russian. And it's not easy. The adjectives were giving me trouble. I came up with a plan. I put a white board up in the office and divided it in half. On the left I wrote "Chris" at the top. On the right I wrote "Jim". You've read about Jim before. At this time he was my back to back – we both did the same job – he did one month; I did the next. And so on. When we handed over, we spent a couple of days together learning Russian.

On the whiteboard, underneath "Chris", I wrote, in Russian, "clever", "wise", "strong", "slim", "friendly", "handsome" … And underneath "Jim", I wrote, in Russian, "stupid", "foolish", "weak", "fat", "difficult", "ugly" …

And during my month at work, whenever a new adjective cropped up, I would add that adjective, and its opposite. My PA gave me a good bollocking – telling me how rude and disrespectful it was. "Rude" and "disrespectful". That gave me two more for "Jim's" list and two more opposites for mine. Cool.

My PA, and some of the other Russians, weren't happy. But I knew Jim well. I knew the first thing he would do was laugh.

And the second thing he would do was swap "Chris" for "Jim" and "Jim" for "Chris". That's exactly what he did and then he carried on adding adjectives during his month at work. First thing I did when I came back, was swap the names again. It was a great little game. "Great" and "Little" – we had those listed of course. Eventually the Russians came to like it. Every time a new adjective came up in conversation, they would put it on the board and it's opposite. Team spirit built, the Russians were laughing, job done.

Usually, when we handed over, there was a couple of hours when neither of us were in the office. The PAs, desperate not to have either Jim or me offended, took to swapping the names over themselves. Whoever arrived new in the office, would find a glowing reference underneath their name on the board.

One of the reasons I went to work in Egypt, was that it was a stable, law abiding place. After Gabon, West Africa, Iran and Siberia, somewhere a bit less challenging, with a bit less bedlam, sounded good. I also wasn't doing a job with direct responsibility for thousands of people – it was much more of a "take a step back", think big and be creative type job. I'd been in Egypt two weeks when Arab Spring I happened, and real bedlam descended on Cairo. Civil insurrection took over from squash as the national sport. Tahrir Square and General Sisi became the answer to quiz questions in every pub in Britain. I'd been in Egypt three weeks when I was evacuated.

I'd been in Egypt three weeks, when I was evacuated.

I wrote before about heliskiing in Kamchatka. The three of us Brits working in Russia, decided to go over to Kamchatka two or three days early. We flew nine time zones East of Moscow and we were still in Russia. We didn't want to start heli-skiing on that kind of jet lag.

We stayed at the stereotypical Soviet style hotel. Where no request was too small to be flatly rejected. Smiling was a crime. Foreigners were the enemy of the state. And there were no guests – only short-term inmates. Don't get me wrong – it was a brilliant experience.

There was a small ski resort – two lifts and three short ski runs – at the edge of Petropavlovsk. Petropavlovsk, the only town in Kamchatka, was a closed area in Soviet times, home of the Northern Pacific fleet, foreigners officially banned at that time. It hadn't really changed that much.

It was 3am Moscow time. We were still definitely on Moscow time. We found a Lada taxi, somehow got the three of us plus our skis in there and went skiing. We knew there'd be very few foreigners in Petropavlovsk. We didn't realise there'd be three. The key to a happy life in Russia, as a foreigner, was to keep a low profile and stay away from bother.

We stood out. There were only a couple of hundred skiers anyway. We had state of the art deep powder skis and bindings. The latest western boot technology. Fluorescent top-quality jackets and trousers. The only three people wearing helmets. We stood out.

After a couple of hours, we'd skied everywhere, on and off piste, that you could get to. We were skiing ever faster as we got familiar with the runs. That wasn't helping with the low profile either. Jim took off down a slope. He was testing his terminal velocity, I think. At a certain point he was on a collision course with another skier. He turned down the slope. As did the other skier. They were then skiing parallel to each other. They stayed neck and neck, about a meter apart. Jim deliberately skiing fast. The other skier – a little bit spooked – went faster and faster. By now they were on the same track, straight down the slope, both on the edge of control, a foot apart.

At a certain point, the other skier's panic took over. They threw their arms around Jim's neck. Locked together they continued down the slope. Jim kept it together for a remarkable distance – presumably to maintain the low profile – full credit for the effort. But eventually the pair collapsed in a pile of skis, sticks, legs and arms. They slid another fifty metres in one large ball of bits.

Jim got up first. Then his new friend. Thankfully both unhurt. The local police chief's daughter. Excellent. All foreigners had to register with the police. We knew we'd be introducing ourselves to her father later that day. We hadn't been banking on the family touch though. That low profile couldn't have been lower really.

Jim got up first. Then his new friend.

Passport control and customs, going into West Africa, could be a bit of an ordeal. Everyone involved in looking at passports, visas and work permits – and there were many – were sizing you up for potential as a get rich quick scheme. The customs officials who looked in every corner of every bag - and there were many – were casing the joint. To coin a phrase.

And every other official, would say, "Do you have something for me?". They were not looking for a smile. The inference was clear, "If you dash me some cash, there'll be no wahalla". My usual reply was that I would love to donate to their pension fund, but I was terribly sorry, and I couldn't. I was avoiding the confrontation of a "no", and the moral dilemma of a "yes" whilst hoping to get through the airport terminal before my next birthday.

I often wondered about the irony. The West Africans in that area were mostly deeply religious people, many with a fervent belief in the most fundamental and orthodox Christian concepts. But with an equally fervent belief that your stuff was there to be nicked, by them. I guess the juxtaposition of religion and poverty.

I travelled with a good friend of mine. A broad Geordie. Brian. He was an enormous bloke, with a big bushy beard and a deep booming voice. It wasn't Brian Blessed, but it could have been his brother. His bigger brother. And louder. Standing behind Brian at the Xray machine, my subconscious heard one of the bag searchers say to him, "Do you have anything for me?". It was so common I was barely aware of it – just tutted inwardly with a sense of "here we go again, I'm back".

In a big loud voice, loud even for Brian, he bellowed, "Yeeeeessssss". I was listening now. He went on, "I have some advice for yooooouuuuu". He pointed up to the ceiling, but gave the customs lady a wide-eyed stare, with a hint of demonic and a pinch of aggression. "He's watching yooooouuuuu". Either Brian was going to be shot, locked up or achieve sainthood. And I wouldn't have bet money on which. Subconsciously I backed away and tried to hide in my bag.

The customs lady visibly shrank. She crossed herself. With a shakey hand she waved him on. Brian picked up his bag and walked unmolested through all further checks. The crowd parted in front of him. An inexplicable ethereal glow followed him. Loaves and fishes self-multiplying in his wake. I offered to carry his bag.

Whenever I travelled into and out of Egypt, I would spend one night in Cairo. We used one specific hotel. It had been built as an old colonial mansion house, by someone who was keen on horse racing. Next to the hotel, and incredibly in the centre of dusty, sandy, Cairo is a full-size oval, grass, horse racing track. Between the track and the hotel there's stabling for two hundred or so horses. And the stables always seemed quite full. On the other side of the hotel was a show jumping arena. There was more stabling with the arena. The hotel had built a lovely upmarket coffee shop overlooking the arena.

The Egyptians have a history of expert horsemanship. In 2012, the arena was being used for training the Egyptian Olympic showjumping team in preparation for London 2012. I had learnt to ride in my twenties and was fairly good. I have what's called, a "hot seat". I can get on pretty much any unwilling, bone idle old nag, and I can generally get it going. On several occasions, I sat in the coffee shop and jealously watched the training in the arena.

The great, the good and the wealthy of Cairo ...

It wasn't just the Olympic team there. There was always someone having showjumping or dressage lessons. The horses were the most beautiful purebred Arab horses. Groomed perfectly. Trained to perfection. As were the riders. Clearly, the great, the good and the wealthy of Cairo, kept their megabuck horses in these stables.

There was a decent fitness centre in the hotel too. I would always be in there for an hour whenever I stayed. The staff were friendly and very helpful. I wondered if it was possible to ride – I was sure it wouldn't be – but why not ask. Hotel reception fobbed me off, I needed to enquire at the fitness centre. So, I did.

Unbelievably, I found that I could wander in, rent a horse and go blasting around the racetrack. Presumably not on Thursday nights, when there was a race on. I fancied a canter around the track looking at central Cairo from a different perspective. But I didn't fancy being chucked off on the far side of the track and walking back without a horse. It was a big track.

I could also have a half hour in the arena for five dollars. They'd even give me a horse, which would be helpful. Or I could go for a ten-session bulk buy for forty dollars. I thought I was hearing things – it would have been twenty times that for those horses in those facilities, in Europe. I went for the bulk buy.

Only trouble was, according to the lady in the fitness centre, that a certain Captain Ahmed would have to see that I could ride. Only then would he let me loose. I could see from her face, that Captain Ahmed had a first name, and it was "bastard". He also didn't speak any English. Matched with my ten words of Arabic, that might be an issue. She was clearly worried that there wouldn't be a common language for Captain Ahmed to be a bastard in, and he wouldn't like that. Her English, as I knew from previous visits to the fitness centre, and this conversation, was perfect. Bless her – she said she'd take me over to Captain Ahmed and help me out.

There is, or was, National Service in Egypt. The army is greatly revered. People are immensely proud of their national service. The officers are all volunteers and drawn from the higher classes of Egyptian society. They typically like to keep their title when they leave the army. So, it wasn't unusual for people at work to introduce themselves as Captain Blah, blah. I don't think they had other ranks – they all seemed to be a Captain Something.

Similarly, university educated engineers, insisted on being called Engineer Fred, or whatever. It is a highly respected status issue. Like being called Doctor Fred in the UK. For the uneducated, but employed, they would be called Mister Fred. Of course, foreign education isn't recognized, so I was always Mister Chris. It was a very subtle, veiled, outwardly polite, but very pointed, insult. Disguised as formal respect.

I could picture Captain Ahmed, as we set off from the fitness centre to meet him. As we walked over to the arena, I realised for the first time that the lady from the fitness centre, was disabled. She had one leg shorter than the other, so walked slowly and with a pronounced limp. Inwardly, I thanked her even more for taking me over.

I stood outside the stables as she went inside to find Captain Ahmed. I was acutely aware that everyone I had ever seen in the arena was equipped to perfection. Shiny riding boots, immaculate jodhpurs, brushed hunting hat, white shirt, tie and dress jacket. I had never worn all that clobber to ride. I didn't have any gear with me at all. I was in running shoes, faded jeans and a t-shirt.

Omar Sharif's more sophisticated brother.

Captain Ahmed appeared. Omar Sharif's more sophisticated brother. Greased black hair, perfectly groomed moustache, starched white shirt, regimental tie, tie pin, jodhpurs and polished boots. Aha. I was introduced as

Mister Chris. He wasn't impressed. He looked down his nose. He said he'd find me a pair of boots, a horse and he'd give me some exercises to do in the arena. Actually, he talked loudly for several minutes. But the lady translating was very polite, and only told me about the boots, the horse and the exercises. 'Nuff said.

Captain Ahmed came back a couple of minutes later. A pair of well-worn boots in one hand. And that unwilling, bone idle, old nag, in the other. The boots would have disappointed a mugger. The horse must have been well hidden at the back of the stables. It hadn't seen the light of day for some time. I wouldn't have known what was older – boots or horse. I'd been put in my place by Captain Ahmed. And it was clear that not only he hadn't finished, but he was looking forward to starting.

I walked the horse into the arena. There was a bit more one-way chat between Captain Ahmed and the fitness lady. Her ears were obviously going to be tired after this. There was no debate who had the authority. He had told the lady she had to stay and translate his instructions. One twitch of the 'tache and she stood to lopsided attention. Literally.

There was a small raised wooden platform in the middle of the arena. The kind of thing the Queen stands on when the household cavalry parade passed. Captain Ahmed and the fitness lady stood on the platform. Captain Ahmed's idea of giving some instructions to see if I could ride, actually meant standing on the wooden platform and bellowing orders. All over the arena I could hear him. I could hear him say something. In Arabic. The fitness lady was quite quietly spoken, however. And I'm a bit deaf. In one ear.

I heard the Arabic and knew an instruction was coming.

Then if I was going the right way for my right, and deaf, ear, to be pointed at the fitness lady, I might hear the translated instruction. But I might not. In which case, I'd just do something. It was a guess what Captain Ahmed was really after. Whatever I did, I did it well. But it had nothing to do with what Captain Ahmed was barking about. He was getting a bit frustrated. A bit like Eric Morecombe on the piano, "I'm playing all the right notes, but not necessarily in the right order".

It probably didn't help that all my chums – there were usually four or five of us staying in the hotel at the same time – had come down to the coffee shop to watch. And encourage. And they weren't quietly spoken.

To get over the volume issue, Captain Ahmed had a brainwave. He told the fitness lady to walk next to the horse. He barked orders from the wooden platform in Arabic. The fitness lady translated it into English as she walked along next to me. And I did whatever she said.

There were two issues though. Her English was excellent. But didn't include any horse riding terms, like trot, or jump, or reins. And the second issue was that every time I went faster than a slow walk, she couldn't keep up. No matter how hard she tried – and she did. Eventually I had Captain Ahmed bellowing from his platform in the middle. And the lady, breathless, mumbling something in English, but from the other side of the arena.

Captain Ahmed's frustration was building to a crescendo. But I've never been that worried about a bit of public humiliation. Eventually I just decided to have a bit of a ride before he exploded and kicked me out. I went through all the paces, changed diagonals, did a few jumps. The fitness lady gave up and Captain Ahmed shut up. The horse really was an unwilling, lazy old nag, but he was doing it. Captain Ahmed wandered off. My chums got louder. That was me barred from the arena. And I still had nine tickets.

That was me barred from the arena. And I still had nine tickets.

Two minutes later Captain Ahmed reappeared. A pair of new shiny boots, a brushed hat, a set of chaps and a riding crop in one hand. A beautifully groomed black Arab thoroughbred in the other.

The fitness lady limped off back to the gym for a lie down. The old nag went back into suspended animation at the back of the stables. Captain Ahmed went off to brush his 'tache. And I had the most fantastic time taking a spirited thoroughbred and myself through our paces in a top-class arena in perfect weather in an iconic location.

I'm saving the nine tickets I've got left. Just in case I run into Captain Ahmed somewhere.

BUCKETS, BABUSHKAS AND BOLLOCKED NAKED

But the biggest bollocking I've ever given, ever seen, ever heard, or ever received, was in Petropavlovsk. In the public banya at Petropavlovsk to be exact. In the warm room to be precise. Not that it is embedded in my head. Not that I still have nightmares about it. Not that I twitch whenever I see a yellow bucket.

After we'd made peace with the police chief and his entire family, we thought we'd keep a low profile at the banya. As you know from my evening with Vitaly the mayor, in his banya, I am a banya afficionado. When faced with a slack afternoon in

189

Petropavlovsk, my vote was for the public banya.

There were no other foreigners in Petropavlovsk. I'm willing to bet there have never been any other foreigners at the public banya. There's a whole banya culture, but I reckoned I knew what was what, and that we'd be able to slip in unnoticed.

Keeping that so important low profile.

"Nyet" The problem we had, was a very practical one. We didn't have towels. I got dispatched to reception of the hotel we were in. The hotel where any request was way too much trouble. I explained in my best Russian with Yorkshirski accent, that we were going to the banya. I knew there were towels behind reception somewhere. But I wasn't absolutely sure there was life behind the eyes of the receptionist I was asking. This request for towels didn't even get a conversation – just a straight "nyet". Clearly beyond comprehension that a hotel might assist its guests. I offered money. But obviously not enough. "Nyet". I asked if they knew where I could buy some towels. "Nyet". I asked if they had many satisfied customers. "Nyet". I'm not easily fobbed off, but on this occasion, I was fobbed. Off. Eventually, to get rid of me, I was told we could get towels at the banya. I knew we couldn't, but I was out of ideas.

The taxi driver was slightly less helpful. But the all-time prize for going above and beyond the call of duty for repelling customers, went to the banya team. We went in the banya building. Paid some money. All men turned right, all women went left. So we did as instructed. We arrived in the cold room for men.

In contrast to Vitali's banya, this cold room was the size of a tennis court. The walls were lined with what can only be described as raised wooden thrones, all joined together, enormous and very ornate. Really, there should have been the knights of King Arthur's court sitting in their allotted thrones. Instead, it looked like dwarfs sitting in normal size high backed wooden chairs. Instead, virtually every throne was occupied by a short, squat, middle-aged, shaven headed, Petropavlovskian hoodlum. From outside we could hear the animated conversation of a big group of blokes, who all knew each other well, putting the world to rights, and taking the piss, at high volume. As we three wandered in, all conversation stopped. We'd been spotted.

We stood in the middle of the room, looking for some spare thrones. Virtually every throne was occupied. Clothes and bags hanging on hooks placed on the wood. The occupants lounging in their assigned throne, smoking, drinking and staring. Naked except for towels around their waists.

There were three empty thrones. On different walls. So, we split up. I said hello to my neighbours. Not a flicker of a smile. I went to shake hands. Nope. General low-level muttering about "innostraniks" – foreigners. Eyes were boring into my back, my front and both sides. As welcomes went, it was a touch frosty.

Back to the centre of the room for a quick conference. Watched by forty pairs of eyes. Lots of muttering. I was a bit less sure I knew what I was doing. Jim's Russian was the best, so he was volunteered to go back to reception and have the rent-a-towel conversation. He wasn't keen. On the way in, the banya receptionist had been clear that she'd done the same charm training as the hotel receptionist. The two of us sat back down in King Arthur's court. Jim wandered off to try and smile the banya receptionist out of her towels.

Five minutes later, he was back. Another meeting in the centre. Same watching, same muttering. He had good news and bad news. Good news was that he'd been sold three towels for ten US each. Result. Bad news was that they were the size of small tea towels. Oh. On cue, the elderly lady who was obviously the cold room attendant, appeared. With three tea towels in her hand. For the foreigners. As she announced. Loudly. To the room in general. The muttering was replaced by chuckling and sniggering. The staring replaced by a bit of pointing. She'd been trying to sell those tea towels for thirty years. And at last three underequipped numpties with cash had wandered in.

... three underequipped numpties with cash ...

Back to our assigned thrones, we stripped off. Staring, muttering, chuckling, pointing. I put on my tea towel mini skirt. It was cunningly one inch too short to go round anyone's waist. Which meant a few inches too short to go round mine. I had a fetching slit up one hip. A hairy Liz Hurley without the safety pins. Since there was no one to chat to, we had another pow-wow in the middle. Staring, muttering, chuckling, pointing. We went to the warm room, hoping for a warmer reception.

The warm room was set up like a small lecture theatre. It had tiered wooden pews. A bit like being in a church on a hill. At the front, on wooden benches, there was a selection of plastic buckets. There were different coloured buckets. The buckets were filled with water. There was a selection of bunches of birch twigs. People were soaking their birch bunches. Other people were coming out of the hot room and chucking a bucket of cold water over themselves. So far, so good. I knew about the buckets and birch. And no one was wearing the funny hat or the nose gear. So, I wasn't going to make any of us look foolish by breaching etiquette. No more than we were doing, by wearing the tea towels.

While we were sitting down in a pew having a pray, we didn't stand out so much. There was less pointing and staring. Less muttering and watching. However, the warm room attendant made the cold room lady look jolly.

There's a generation of soviet era Russian women, who hate everything. And everyone. They are generally built like wrestlers. They bristle with antipathy and aggression. The uniform is a blue nylon dress. And slippers. They migrated into customer service jobs because a career in executions had been abolished, and a career in the police, military or as a hoodlum, didn't give them enough of an outlet for their natural pent-up fury. They love rules – the more confusing and unworkable the better. They are of a certain age – fifties and sixties. They like, should we say, eating pies. And people. They all have brass teeth. There must have been a run on dental brass in the seventies and eighties. They are termed "babushkas".

The bolshy bunch in the cool room, that had us quivering with fear, turned into compliant little lambs when faced with the warm room babushka. We picked up some water-soaked birch bunches and went into the hot room. Babushka took one look at the tea towels. The look let us know we'd been marked out for special attention. We were safe in the hot room though. It was so hot that everyone was concentrating too much on staying alive to take any notice of the tea towel team. We did a load of mutual whipping and I treated everyone to an authentic

Too hot for the devil.

Siberian groan or two. Everyone was in a good mood in there. United against the common enemy – heat like the bowels of hell. We were all unsupervised - Babushka obviously didn't come in there. Too hot for the devil.

We lasted a few minutes, and delighted not to have spontaneously combusted, we headed back for the warm room. Sitting up high in the pews, we people watched a bit. Then I got adventurous. I knew I shouldn't have done. I decided to go and pour a bucket of cold water over myself down at the front. Lots of people had done it. I minced down the steps, maintaining dignity with my thigh split, in the direction of the buckets. I was aware of eyes watching. Including babushka's laser glare. I got to the front, and confident I understood protocol, picked up a yellow bucket and poured the contents over my head.

There was an eruption over my left shoulder. Somewhere between a bellowing bear and a charging rhino. I cringed a bit thinking the roof was collapsing or it was the first shockwave from an earthquake. Another bellow, but this time I was being beaten with birch twigs. I dropped my tea towel in fright. I'd been beaten with birch twigs before, but this was a beating born of genuine loathing. The noise hadn't stopped, and I could see that the rhino bellow was coming from behind the brass teeth.

... waiting thirty years for someone to fuck up.

I know the tea towel wasn't recognized banya fashion, but apart from being a foreigner, I didn't know what capital crime I'd committed. The Babushka had been working at the banya for two or three lifetimes. She had ruled the bolshy bunch in the warm room with an iron fist. She had seen it all. She had been waiting thirty years for someone to fuck up. And it was me. She beat me out of the warm room, back into the cool room. Chasing me the whole way with birch twigs, buckets and hatred – ranting at peak volume. Brass teeth snarling. She slammed the door behind me and suddenly it was quiet. I looked up wondering if I was safe.

The forty or so blokes on the thrones, and in the towels, sitting around the walls of the cool room, were looking at me in total silence. I took my hands off my head. As I did, the door opened again. Babushka threw my tea towel at me and had a final rant. She slammed the door shut again.

Head down, I trudged back to my throne. And sat down. The neighbour on my left, reached out his hand and shook mine. The neighbour on my right, gave me a beer. They all smiled warmly in my direction. The camaraderie of a near death experience *...both barrels of babushka* shared. I think they'd been running a book on which of the three of us would get both barrels of Babushka.

My crime? Yellow buckets were for soaking birch twigs. Blue buckets were for tipping over your head. For the second time in two days, no one would have known there were foreigners in town.

THE END

SINCE I LEFT Oil and Gas Inc. (International), skipping out of the door, I've been busy. Technical lecturing at a University. Technical stuff with a few Oil and Gas consultancies. Some pro bono work. A couple of yacht deliveries. Preparing for the 2022/23 Clipper Race – if that takes thirty years, we've taken a wrong turn.

And many miles running, cycling and swimming. Therefore, lots of thinking. And a few great ideas. And this book.

But I've been more in demand as a coach, than for technical work. Coaching new oilfield leaders through technical, commercial, business, safety and leadership dilemmas. And now coaching leaders outside the oil and gas arena. These are welcome challenges that truly inspire me.

Story telling is a little used, but hugely powerful technique, for coaching. Of course, you have to have the library of stories. Which is where most leadership coaches lack credibility - never led anything, anywhere, in adversity, of any significance.

In the course of retelling the stories in this book, I realised that I have a fund of stories that would help me coach leaders. None of those stories are in this book.

This book is full of simple, light-hearted experiences that are generally an easy read. Recalling the stuff that has made me laugh, while learning about human behaviour in different cultures when people, including me, are … "cold, tired, hungry, far from home, on your thirtieth straight day working, under pressure, frightened and pissed off – as you are frequently in the oilfield – don't judge."

There are an equal number of semi-technical or business-related stories that are edgier, harder to write and even harder to read. Considerably more poignant. Reflecting on the toughest of oil field dilemmas and setbacks. Sometimes sad. Sometimes with human cost. But all with real potential to help leaders develop themselves, their teams and their business.

Anywhere you have thousands of people, from multiple cultures, using several languages, in a high risk industry, in hostile places, in challenging environments and working under pressure, every technical and human dilemma you can imagine will walk into the office. And many dilemmas that you could never imagine. Every day a bizarre event – just didn't know what it was going to be.

I'm sure I can fill a second book with these leadership learning opportunities, and use it as a coaching aid.

In the meantime, congratulations on getting to the end of this book. I hope you have laughed. Unless you've flicked straight to The End. In which case, go back and read it properly. It's good shit.

Comments, suggestions and criticism welcome. Don't be shy. Justforastart@gmail.com.

(

Printed in Great Britain
by Amazon